DISCARDED

THE HAWAIIAN INCIDENT

THE HAWAIIAN INCIDENT

AN EXAMINATION

OF

MR. CLEVELAND'S ATTITUDE

TOWARD THE

REVOLUTION OF 1893

BY

J. A. GILLIS

BOOKS FOR LIBRARIES PRESS
FREEPORT, NEW YORK

First Published 1897
Reprinted 1970

STANDARD BOOK NUMBER:
8369-5331-2

LIBRARY OF CONGRESS CATALOG CARD NUMBER:
77-117878

PRINTED IN THE UNITED STATES OF AMERICA

THE HAWAIIAN INCIDENT

No act of Mr. Cleveland's administration has met with such severe criticism as the course which he adopted toward the Sandwich Islands at the time of the dethronement of the Queen in 1893. No epithets have seemed sufficient to characterize his "base and ignoble policy" — a policy claimed to have been unscrupulous in itself, and opposed to all republican and democratic ideas. So constant has been the abuse lavished upon Mr. Cleveland, so persistent has been the misrepresentation of facts, that not only those of opposite politics have believed the charges against him, but some of those who have supported him in general, have thought that there must have been some cause for the abuse so freely bestowed, and have supposed that there was at least one blot upon a record otherwise unblemished.

It is intended to make some suggestions as to the real character of the proceedings in question. It is not proposed, of course, to make an exhaustive inquiry into the events preceding the so-called "revolution" resulting in the overthrow of the Queen's government, nor to ask whether this government was a good or bad one, or whether the action of the Queen was such as to justify her dethronement. To do that would require too great a space and might prove a weariness to the reader; but attention will be called to the letters and statements of the parties active in the overturn of the Hawaiian throne, which will show that this event occurred with the connivance and assistance of the American minister and was aided by the presence in Honolulu of United States troops, who were called on shore from the United States ship "Boston," then lying in the harbor, ostensibly for the purpose of protecting life and property, but really for the purpose of protecting the revolutionists, while the "revolution" was going on. It will be specially noticed that the letters and statements which are relied upon to show this will be those of the chief actors, or of those whose interests lay upon their side; some testimony of the officers of the United States navy will be offered, but otherwise no statements of those interested upon the Queen's side, nor even of those who might be fairly regarded as disinterested, will be presented. No special effort will be made to defend or explain Mr. Cleveland's action, except by offering the facts as gathered in the manner alluded to, and by showing what that action was; and the reader will form his own judgment as to whether or not Mr. Cleveland's course was controlled by reason and justice, and dictated by a true regard for American honor.

In February, 1893, a report was made upon the following resolution of the United States Senate:

Resolved, That the Committee on Foreign Relations shall inquire and report whether any, and, if so, what, irregularities have occurred in the diplomatic or other intercourse between the United States and Hawaii in relation to the recent political revolution in Hawaii, and to this end said committee is authorized to send for persons and papers and to administer oaths to witnesses.

This report is published as a public document, entitled "Hawaiian Islands. Report of the Committee of Foreign Relations, United States Senate, with accompanying documents,"[1] in two volumes, which contain also the testimony

---

[1] The figures in the text refer to a list at the close of this volume, in which references are made to the pages of this Report.

taken before the committee, that taken by Mr. Blount in Honolulu, and various papers, official and otherwise, pertaining to the Hawaiian Islands.

It is unnecessary to say that the statements made by the parties testifying on the one side and the other are wholly contradictory upon nearly every important point.

In order to understand the course of events at Honolulu it is necessary to take into view the ideas and sentiments of Mr. John L. Stevens, the United States minister at the Sandwich Islands. It will appear most clearly that Mr. Stevens regarded himself as having a mission, that mission being to bring about the annexation of the islands to the United States, which he was ready to promote and recommend at all times and seasons. To show this a few citations will be given. He was appointed in June, 1889, and arrived in Honolulu on the twentieth of September of that year, and on the seventh of October he writes to Mr. Blaine :[1]

I am much impressed by the strong American feeling pervading the best portion of the population, and which is especially manifest among the men of business and property.

On the 20th of March, 1890, he writes again to Mr. Blaine :[2]

The actions of the department of State afford conclusive evidence of the interest which the government of the United States has long taken in the affairs of the Hawaiian Islands. That these tendencies are of great importance to the future development and defence of American commerce in the Pacific hardly will be questioned. To secure the influence over them which the United States so long has considered its right and duty to maintain, some decisive steps must soon be taken which, in the past, were not of pressing necessity. For more than half a century the American Missionary Board, with the agencies and influences in its control, has served as a strong fortress to the United States in these islands. The large financial contributions, amounting to nearly one million of dollars, which that organization obtained through innumerable channels of American benevolence and religious zeal, and the large number of educated and resolute agents which it sent to these islands, secured an influence over the ruling chiefs and native population which held them as firmly to America as a permanent military force could have done.

But a change of facts and circumstances in recent years is bringing near the time when this well-sustained power must be strongly reënforced. In a large and increasing degree other influences have come in to counterbalance and relatively to decrease the American missionary influences.

. . . .

Shall American civilization ultimately prevail here? The near future is to show conclusively that only the strong pressure and continual vigilance of the United States can enable American men and American ideas to hold ascendency here and make these islands as prosperous and valuable to American commerce, and to American marine supremacy in the North Pacific, as the isles of the Mediterranean have been and are to its adjacent nations.

On the 20th of August, 1891, he writes: [3]

The best security in the future, and the only permanent security, will be the moral pressure of the business men and of what are termed "the missionary people," and the presence in the harbor of Honolulu of an American man-of-war.

. . . .

But as early as the first of December, without fail, the month preceding the election, and for sometime thereafter, there should be a United States vessel here to render things secure. I have strong reluctance to being regarded an alarmist, but with due regard to my responsibility I am impelled to express the opinion that a proper regard for American interests will require one ship here most of the time in 1892.

On the 8th of February, 1892, he writes: [4]

There are increasing indications that the annexation sentiment is growing among the business men, as well as with the less responsible of the foreign and native population of the islands. The present political situation is feverish, and I see no prospect of its being permanently otherwise until these islands become a part of the American Union or a possession of Great Britain.

. . . .

At a future time, after the proposed treaty shall have been ratified, I shall deem it my official duty to give a more elaborate statement of facts and reasons why a "new departure" by the United States as to Hawaii is rapidly becoming a necessity, that a "protectorate" is impracticable, and that annexation must be the future remedy, or else Great Britain will be furnished with circumstances and opportunity to get a hold on these islands which will cause future serious embarrassment to the United States.

Again in a long and elaborate letter to Mr. Foster, Secretary of State under Mr. Harrison's administration, we have the following:[5]

[*Confidential.*]

UNITED STATES LEGATION,
HONOLULU, Nov. 20, 1892.

SIR: Fidelity to the trust imposed on me by the President, the Department of State, and the Senate requires that I should make a careful and full statement of the financial, agricultural, social, and political condition of these islands. An intelligent and impartial examination of the facts can hardly fail to lead to the conclusion that the relations and policy of the United States toward Hawaii will soon demand some change, if not the adoption of decisive measures, with the aim to secure American interests and future supremacy by encouraging Hawaiian development and aiding to promote responsible government in these islands.

. . . .

Directly and indirectly, the palace probably costs the little kingdom $150,000 per year. A governor, at $5,000 a year, acting in harmony with the responsible men of the Legislature, would be far better for the islands than the present monarchical Government. In truth, the monarchy here is an absurd anachronism. It has nothing on which it logically or legitimately stands.

. . . .

As a crown colony of Great Britain, or a territory of the United States, the Government modifications could be made readily, and good administration of the laws secured. Destiny and the vast future interests of the United States in the Pacific clearly indicate who, at no distant day, must be responsible for the government of these islands. Under a territorial government they could be as easily governed as any of the existing territories of the United States.

The men qualified are here to carry on good government, provided they have the support of the Government of the United States. Why not postpone American possession? Would it not be just as well for the United States to take the islands twenty-five years hence? Facts and obvious probabilities will answer both of these interrogations. Hawaii has reached the parting of the ways. She must now take the road which leads to Asia, or the other, which outlets her in America, gives her an American civilization, and binds her to the care of American destiny.

. . . .

To postpone American action many years is only to add to present unfavorable tendencies and to make future possession more difficult.

Then, after pointing out the injury to the sugar planters by reason of the McKinley bill, he says:

Unless some positive measures of relief be granted, the depreciation of sugar property here will continue to go on. Wise, bold action of the United States will rescue the property-holders from great loss, give the islands a government which will put an end to a worse than useless expenditure of a large proportion of the revenues of the country, using them for the building of roads and bridges, thus helping to develop the natural resources of the islands, aiding to diversify the industries, and to increase the number of the responsible citizens. One of two courses seems to me absolutely necessary to be followed: either bold and vigorous measures for annexation or a "customs union," an ocean cable from the Californian coast to Honolulu, Pearl harbor perpetually ceded to the United States, with an implied but not necessarily stipulated American protectorate over the islands. I believe the former to be the better, that which will prove much the more advantageous to the islands, and the cheapest and least embarrassing in the end for the United States.

. . . .

To-day the United States has five times the wealth she possessed in 1854, and the reasons now existing for annexation are much stronger than they were then. I cannot refrain from expressing the opinion with emphasis that the golden hour is near at hand.

. . . .

So long as the islands retain their own independent government there remains the possibility that England or the Canadian Dominion might secure one of the Hawaiian harbors for a coaling station. Annexation excludes all dangers of this kind.

Which of the two lines of policy and action shall be adopted, our statesmen and Government must decide. Certain it is that the interests of the United States and the welfare of these islands will not permit the continuance of the existing state and tendency of things. Having for so many years extended a helping hand to the islands and encouraging the American residents and their friends at home to the extent we have, we cannot refrain now from aiding them with vigorous measures, without injury to ourselves and those of our "kith and kin," and without neglecting American opportunities that never seemed so obvious and pressing as they do now. I have no doubt that the more thoroughly the bed-rock and controlling facts touching the Hawaiian problem are understood by our Government and by the American public, the more readily they will be inclined to approve the views I have expressed so inadequately in this communication.

In a letter to Mr. Foster, Jan. 18, 1893 (the day after the revolution), having given an account of the transactions of the 16th, he writes as follows: [6]

All is quiet here now. Without the sacrifice of a single life this change of government has been accomplished. Language can hardly express the enthusiasm and the profound feeling of relief at this peaceful and salutary change of government. The underlying cause of this profound feeling among the citizens is the hope that the United States Government will allow these islands to pass to American control and become American soil. A commission of citizens, duly accredited, will go by the steamer that takes this despatch to Washington, to state the wishes of the Provisional Government and of the responsible people of the islands, and to give a complete account of the existing state of things here.

And February 1, he writes: [7] "The Hawaiian pear is now fully ripe, and this is the golden hour for the United States to pluck it." Finally, in the "North American Review" for December, 1893, Mr. Stevens winds up a long article in favor of annexation as follows:

To say that we do not need the Hawaiian Islands as a security to our immense future interests is but the babble of children or incompetent men. It is blindly and recklessly to ignore the logic of inimitable circumstances and to scoff at the plainest teachings of history. No! America cannot get rid of her future responsibilities if she would, and all attempts to do so will be at the cost of her future generations. In the light of these inexorable truths of what is most sacred in Christian civilization, in behalf of a noble American colony holding the advanced post of America's progress, I cherish the faith that the American people, the American statesmen, thoughtful of America's great future, will settle the Hawaiian question wisely and well — will see to it that the flag of the United States floats unmolested over the Hawaiian Islands.

Mr. Stevens's sentiments in regard to the Queen were no less pronounced than those in reference to annexation. As early as April 2, 1892, he begins to speak of her in the most disparaging terms. He says, " For twenty years the palace has been the centre of corruption and scandal, and is likely to remain so as long as the Hawaiian monarch exists."

His official correspondence is filled with remarks (which need not be quoted here) reflecting upon the Queen's private character, and indeed he finds it difficult to speak of her without some derogatory allusion.[1] In his examination before the Congressional committee he makes these references time after time; he mentions the "semi-barbaric Queen" and her "semi-barbaric court," and in speaking of her signing "iniquitous bills" he says, " Both she and the ring of adventurers who surrounded her expected there would thus be established a scheme to rob the people of millions of money." These expressions of Mr. Stevens's, both in regard to annexation and to the Queen, are here brought forward, not for the purpose of praise or blame, but that the reader may judge of his

---

[1] Thus, for instance, in his letter of Oct. 19, 1892, he makes three, and in that of Oct. 31, 1892, four allusions of this kind.

state of mind, and may form an opinion as to what he would be likely to do in a contingency to which he refers in a letter which is now to be quoted.

This letter to Mr. Blaine is dated March 8, 1892, about ten months before the Queen was dethroned, and commenced as follows: [8]

UNITED STATES LEGATION,
HONOLULU, March 8, 1892.

SIR: In view of possible contingencies in these islands, I ask for the instructions of the Department of State on the following, viz.:

If the Government here should be surprised and overturned by an orderly and peaceful revolutionary movement, largely of native Hawaiians, and a provisional or republican government organized and proclaimed, would the United States minister and naval commander here be justified in responding affirmatively to the call of the members of the removed Government to restore them to power or replace them in possession of the Government buildings? Or should the United States minister and naval commander confine themselves exclusively to the preservation of American property, the protection of American citizens, and the prevention of anarchy? Should a revolutionary attempt of the character indicated be made, there are strong reasons to presume that it would begin with the seizure of the police-station, with its arms and ammunition, and this accomplished, the Royal Palace and the Government building, containing the cabinet offices and archives, would very soon be captured, the latter building being situated about one-third of a mile from the police-station. In such contingencies, would it be justifiable to use the United States forces here to restore the Government buildings to the possession of the displaced officials? Ordinarily in like circumstances the rule seems to be to limit the landing and movement of the United States force in foreign waters and dominion exclusively to the protection of the United States legation, and of the lives and property of American citizens. But as the relations of the United States to Hawaii are exceptional, and in former years the United States officials here took somewhat exceptional action in circumstances of disorder, I desire to know how far the present minister and naval commander may deviate from established international rules and precedents in the contingencies indicated in the first part of this despatch.

It is not claimed that the revolution, foreshadowed in the above remarkable letter, was the one now in question, because the latter arose suddenly and upon an unexpected opportunity, but this letter is of great importance for several reasons: First, it shows that nearly a year before the events in question, and while the Queen was reigning in perfect peace and amity with the country which he represented, Mr. Stevens was contemplating the possibility of the surprise and overturn of the Government by "an orderly and peaceful revolutionary movement" (whatever that may mean), and was considering and inquiring whether he and the naval commander would be "justified" in restoring the Government, or whether they should "confine themselves exclusively" to protection of American citizens and property and prevention of anarchy, being apparently in doubt which course should be pursued. Secondly, it points out what would be the "ordinary" rule; but as (in his mind) the relations of the United States to Hawaii are exceptional, he wishes to know how far he and the naval commander may "deviate" from established international rules and precedent in the contingency named. The meaning of this suggested "deviation" will become more clear as we proceed.

Finally, this letter practically writes in advance the history of the present revolutionary movement, but with one very important variation. Mr. Stevens, looking to the future, and considering the course a revolution would be likely to take, presumes that it would begin with the seizure of the police-station with its arms and ammunition, which being accomplished, the remaining work would soon be done. The possession of the station-house would be an absolute prerequisite to a successful revolution, and it would naturally be the first point of attack. But the noticeable thing is that when the present revolution was attempted, the possession of the station-house, in which were the Queen's troops, with their arms and ammunition, becomes a matter of no importance, and Mr. Stevens was ready and willing to recognize a set of men who had possession of the Government buildings only. This will be amply shown by his own letters, and it is very important to this inquiry that his attitude, as taken in this letter of March 8, ten months before the revolution, should be noticed and remembered when his subsequent acts and letters are examined.

In 1893 the government of the Sandwich Islands was a constitutional monarchy. At the head was Queen Liliuokalani; there was a Cabinet consisting of four ministers, and a Legislature consisting of twenty-four members of the House of Nobles, and twenty-four representatives of the people. Members of both Houses were elected by popular vote, an educational qualification being necessary for all voters, and a property qualification for electors for nobles. The constitution then in force was adopted in 1887.

Upon the fourteenth day of January, 1893, being Saturday, the Queen, for various reasons which need not be considered here, proposed to promulgate, and took some steps towards promulgating, a new constitution; an attempt which was no doubt in violation of the constitution then existing. More or less excitement and opposition resulted, and the attempt was abandoned; and on Monday notice to this effect was given, and at or about noon the following printed proclamation was circulated through the city: [9]

BY AUTHORITY.

Her Majesty's ministers desire to express their appreciation for the quiet and order which has prevailed in this community since the events of Saturday, and are authorized to say that the position taken by Her Majesty in regard to the promulgation of a new constitution was under the stress of her native subjects. Authority is given for the assurance that any changes desired in the fundamental law of the land will be sought only by methods provided in the constitution itself. Her Majesty's ministers request all citizens to accept the assurance of Her Majesty in the same spirit in which it is given.

LILIUOKALANI.
SAMUEL PARKER,
Minister of Foreign Affairs.
W. H. CORNWELL,
Minister of Finance.
JOHN F. COLBURN,
Minister of the Interior.
A. P. PETERSON,
Attorney-General.

IOLANI PALACE, Jan. 16, 1893.

In the meantime, on Saturday the 14th,[10] some persons met at the office of Mr. W. O. Smith, a prominent lawyer of Honolulu, and after some discussion organized themselves as a meeting, of which Mr. Smith was secretary, and a committee of nine, afterwards increased to thirteen, was appointed to form plans for action, call meetings, report any time at their discretion, and be called a Committee of Safety.

It is asserted that at that time there was some serious apprehension that disorder might follow the attempt of the Queen to promulgate the new constitution; that there was an intense feeling of uncertainty, and a fear that danger to the community was very imminent.

The claim has been made throughout by Mr. Stevens and the parties engaged in the movement that the action of the Queen caused great consternation, that there were grave apprehensions of disorder and riot, and that there was great cause to believe that life and property were in danger. Thus Mr. W. C. Wilder says:[11]

At the request of many citizens, whose wives and families were helpless and in terror of an expected uprising of the mob, which would burn and destroy, a request was made and signed by all of the committee, addressed to Minister Stevens, that troops might be landed to protect houses and private property.

All this is denied upon the other side, who claim that the city was amply protected and perfectly safe, and they describe the condition of affairs in much detail. Fortunately we have a test, as will be seen hereafter, in the actions of the revolutionists themselves, as to what was their real belief upon this subject.

The following supplementary statement made to the Committee on Foreign Relations, by Mr. C. Bolte, who, as well as Mr. W. C. Wilder to whom he refers, was a member of the Committee of Safety and of the Provisional Government, will perhaps show whether these two gentlemen and others were overwhelmed with consternation, or whether they welcomed with enthusiasm the advent of the golden opportunity: [12]

The answers which I have given to Mr. Blount's question, "When was for the first time anything said about deposing or dethroning the Queen?" might lead to misunderstanding in reading this report. I desire, therefore, to hereby declare as follows: Words to the effect that the Queen must be deposed or dethroned were not uttered to my knowledge at any meeting of the Committee of Safety until Monday evening, Jan. 16, 1893; but at the very first meeting of citizens at W. O. Smith's office on Saturday, January 14, at about 2 P.M., or even before this meeting had come to order, Paul Neumann informed the arriving people that the Queen was about to promulgate a new constitution. The answer then given him by Mr. W. C. Wilder, by me, and by others was: That is a very good thing and a splendid opportunity to get rid of the whole old rotten Government concern and now to get annexation to the United States. Paul Neumann thought that that might be going a little too far.

At the second meeting at W. O. Smith's, between 3 and 4 P.M. on Saturday afternoon, Jan. 14, 1893, when the Committee of Safety was appointed, sentiments of the same nature, that this is a splendid opportunity to get rid of the old *régime*, and strong demands for annexation, or any kind of stable government under the supervision of the United States, were expressed.

Therefore, even if the words that the Queen must be deposed or dethroned were not spoken, surely the sentiment that this must be done prevailed at or even before the very first meeting, on Jan. 14, 1893.

Mr. Stevens had been absent from Honolulu for about ten days on a trip to Hilo, one of the Hawaiian Islands, in the United States ship-of-war "Boston," and returned on Saturday, January 14, the day when the proceedings in question commenced; and communication was at once opened with him by the revolutionists, and was continued from day to day, as the progress of events is traced in the statements of the revolutionists themselves.

Attention is now asked to the following extracts from the statement of Mr. W. O. Smith, at whose office a meeting had been organized, as stated above, and a committee of thirteen, to be called a Committee of Safety, appointed. After giving the names of the committee, he says: [13]

> After further delay, almost immediately the others present were requested to retire, and the committee held a meeting. The situation was briefly discussed — the imminence of danger and the safety of the city; what action should be taken for protection was the main subject of discussion. And in view of the fact that at the station-house there was a large armed force, and at the barracks, and that nearly all of the arms were in possession of the supporters of the Queen, and there was no organization at the time outside of those forces, and it was simply unknown how many arms were available, the question was at once discussed whether a protectorate should not be sought from the United States steamship-of-war "Boston;" that question was, of course, first raised, whether the United States would render assistance, or what their attitude would be, and then a special committee, consisting of L. A. Thurston, W. C. Wilder, and H. F. Glade, were appointed to wait upon Mr. J. L. Stevens, United States minister, and inform him of the situation, and ascertain from him what, if any, protection or assistance could be afforded by the United States forces for the protection of life and property, the unanimous sentiment and feeling being that life and property were in imminent danger. By that time it was so dark that I lighted the electric light. We had to have light before we concluded our meeting and deliberations.

. . . .

The probabilities of what the Queen would do were discussed; there was no certainty in regard to that, excepting that she would undoubtedly persist in her revolutionary intentions; what would be done, how soon martial law might be declared, or any other course would be taken, what steps would be taken, we simply could not tell, and after discussion Mr. Thurston made the following motion: "That steps be taken at once to form and declare a Provisional Government."

The seriousness of the step was considered, but it was decided unanimously by the committee that some such steps had got to be taken for protection of life and property, and it was then, and after Mr. Cooper's statement in regard to his visit to the "Boston," that the committee consisting of Thurston, Wilder, and Glade were appointed to meet the American minister, and were instructed to report the next morning at 9 o'clock, at a meeting to be called at the residence of W. R. Castle.

I went home about dark or a little after, and just had dinner, when Mr. Thurston called at my house on his way home, asking me to meet the committee and one or two others at his house at 8 o'clock. I went there and found Mr. Thurston, W. R. Castle, F. W. Wundenberg, A. S. Hartwell, S. B. Dole, and C. L. Carter. Mr. Thurston stated that the committee had waited upon the American minister, and that he had said that the United States troops on board the "Boston" would be ready to land any moment to prevent the destruction of American life and property, and in regard to the matter of establishing a Provisional Government, they of course would recognize the existing Government whatever it might be.

Mr. Thurston stated to Mr. Stevens the proposition that was under consideration, of establishing a Provisional Government, and in case those steps were taken, he asked Mr. Stevens what his attitude would be, and Mr. Stevens had told him whatever Government was established, and was actually in possession of the Government building, the executive departments and archives, and *in possession of the city,* that was a *de facto* Government proclaiming itself as a Government, would necessarily have to be recognized. Everything had culminated in a few hours, we were laboring under intense feeling, and it was arranged that different ones of those present should begin drafting papers. Mr. W. R. Castle undertook to draft something in the nature of a brief historical statement, which would be for a preamble to the declaration. Mr. Thurston was to work upon the matter of the form of the Provisional Government. Judge Dole quietly stated that he was not prepared to take part in the movement, but that he would assist, at Mr. Thurston's request, in drafting the declaration. I was requested to draft papers to be submitted to the American minister requesting the landing of the troops, in case it became necessary. At a late hour we retired, and the next morning at 9 o'clock the committee of thirteen met at W. R. Castle's residence.

The meeting continued until noon. The committee appointed to wait on the American minister made a report to the committee similar to the report made to us the night before. Among the various propositions and matters discussed was a matter of calling a public mass meeting, and it was decided to call a meeting at 2 o'clock in the afternoon of the next day, Monday, to be held, if possible, at the old rifle armory on Beretania street, near the corner of Punchbowl street.

. . . .

At the meeting at Mr. Castle's there was considerable discussion in regard to when to have the mass meeting; some were in favor of having it on Sunday; a feeling, too, had been expressed at the meeting on Saturday afternoon that there should be a mass meeting called, and it was finally decided to hold it at 2 o'clock Monday.

. . . .

At that meeting [at Mr. Castle's], and the previous and subsequent meetings, most meagre minutes were kept, because of the possible danger of our being arrested, and of these records being used against us. The night before, Mr. Thurston requested Mr. Wundenberg to ascertain, as far as he could, what arms were available and how many men could be depended upon. Just at the close of the meeting Mr. Wundenberg came in with Mr. Soper, and they reported that the prospect of obtaining arms was very discouraging, but that after making a thorough search of the town only about sixty stand of arms were found that were not in possession of the Government.[1]

After we adjourned, Mr. Thurston and I called upon the American minister again and informed him of what was being done. Among other things we talked over with him what had better be done in case of our being arrested, or extreme or violent measures being taken by the monarchy in regard to us. We did not know what steps would be taken, and there was a feeling of great unrest and sense of danger in the community. Mr. Stevens gave assurance of his earnest purpose to afford all the protection that was in his power to protect life and

---

[1] *i.e.*, the Queen's Government.

property; he explained the fact that, while he would call for the United States troops to protect life and property, he would not recognize any government until actually established.

Sunday evening several of the parties met at Mr. Thurston's house. The next morning, Monday, January 16, there was a meeting of the whole committee at Mr. Thurston's office.[14] At this meeting a committee of five was appointed to wait upon the Queen's ministers, who had requested to see them. Mr. Smith resumes:

The committee of five returned and reported that they had met the four ministers, and the ministers stated to them that they had no communication to make, and wanted to know what the committee wanted. They talked over the situation and showed our committee a proclamation signed by the Queen and the ministers, stating that she would never again attempt to force a new constitution. Before the meeting broke up the form of the request to the American minister in regard to the landing of the troops was adopted and signed by the committee of thirteen, requesting the American minister to land troops, and this request was signed by the committee of thirteen, and decided to be delivered to the minister to be held by him, but not to be acted upon until a further request was received from the committee.

Then, after speaking of the mass meeting, at which he says there was a very large number of people, and at which Mr. Thurston spoke, he goes on:

There was a short and earnest discussion of what was to be done; it was then nearly 4; our plans had not been perfected, papers had not been completed, and after a hasty discussion, the time being very short, it was decided that it was impossible for us to take the necessary steps, and we should request that the troops be not landed until next morning, the hour in the morning being immaterial, whether it was 9 or 8 or 6 o'clock in the morning, but we must have further time to prevent bloodshed, and Mr. Thurston and I were appointed to proceed at once to the American minister and inform him of our decision. We proceeded at once to Mr. Stevens's house, the United States Legation, stated the case to him, and he said that as a precautionary measure, and to protect American life and property, he had ordered the troops to be landed at 5 o'clock, and that they would come. It was then decided to adjourn to meet at the house of Henry Waterhouse at 8 o'clock in the evening. The meeting broke up, and some of us went down to see the troops landed. Thurston gave up — sick. He had to go to bed.

At 8 o'clock in the evening we met at Mr. Henry Waterhouse's. All of the members of the committee were present except Thurston, Castle, and Wilder, they all being ill. Mr. James B. Castle was present, taking the place of W. R. Castle, and C. L. Carter taking the place of Thurston. There were also present by invitation Alexander Young, J. H. Soper, Cecil Brown, H. P. Baldwin, and F. W. Wundenberg.

Previous to this meeting, beginning with the meeting on Saturday afternoon, the suggestion of sending the "Claudine" to San Francisco with despatches to the United States Government was discussed, and at this meeting Monday evening it was moved that she be sent at once to San Francisco. The motion was amended that action be deferred until after the establishment of the Provisional Government. Amendment carried.

At 10 o'clock the next day, January 17, the committee met at the office of W. O. Smith; and Mr. C. L. Carter, on behalf of the committee, reported the names of those who had consented to go upon the Executive and Advisory Councils. It was voted that the Advisory Committee be increased from eight to thirteen, and additional names be suggested to the committee from whom they could select the five additional names. Various names were suggested. It was voted that the committee request Mr. Wilder to report if the "Claudine" could be chartered to go to San Francisco and at what cost. It was voted that the inter-island steamship companies be requested not to allow any vessels to leave for the other islands before 10 o'clock on the next day. At 11 o'clock the judge [S. B. Dole] came before the committee and stated that he would accept the position as chairman of the Executive Council.

Then, after giving the names of the persons there, Mr. Smith adds: "During the meeting in the forenoon, Mr. S. M. Damon came in and reported that he had had an interview with the Queen in which he had advised her not to make resistance, but to submit, and that she would have every opportunity for presenting her claims."

Thus we learn, among other things, that immediately upon the formation of the Committee of Safety, and before any action whatever had been taken, the first thing thought of was the United States troops, the point being at once raised and discussed as to seeking a protectorate from the ship-of-war "Boston;" that a special committee of three was immediately appointed to wait upon Mr. Stevens, inform him of the situation, and ask what he would do; that on that first day (Saturday), before 8 o'clock in the evening, that committee had seen Mr. Stevens, and that a report of their conference with him was made by the special committee at a meeting of the Committee of Safety holden at Mr. Castle's house at 9 o'clock Sunday morning; that after this meeting adjourned, Mr. Thurston and Mr. Smith again called upon Mr. Stevens and informed him of what was being done, and talked over with him what should be done in case of their arrest; and, finally, that after a mass meeting a sub-committee was appointed to call upon Mr. Stevens, with the request that the troops should not be landed that night, the request, however, coming a little too late, as he had already directed the troops to be brought on shore.

Mr. Smith's highly significant statement in regard to the large armed force at the station-house and barracks, and the fact that nearly all the arms were in the hands of the Queen's supporters, will not be overlooked.

The following is the request which the committee had drawn up. It will be noticed that it appeals to the minister and the United States forces for assistance, and while it speaks of general alarm and terror it does not use the formula "protection for life and property," but asks for assistance and protection for "ourselves." It will be seen also what confidential relations existed between Mr. Stevens and the committee, when it appears that this most important paper was to be left in Mr. Stevens's hands, but action was not to be taken upon it till the committee should see fit to make a further request: [15]

CITIZENS' COMMITTEE OF SAFETY TO MR. STEVENS.

HAWAIIAN ISLANDS, HONOLULU, Jan. 16, 1893.

SIR: We, the undersigned, citizens and residents of Honolulu, respectfully represent that in view of recent public events in this kingdom, culminating in the revolutionary acts of Queen Lilioukalani on Saturday last, the public safety is menaced and lives and property are in peril, and we appeal to you and the United States forces at your command for assistance.

The Queen, with the aid of armed force, and accompanied by threats of violence and bloodshed from those with whom she was acting, attempted to proclaim a new constitution; and, while prevented for the time from accomplishing her object, declared publicly that she would only defer her action.

This conduct and action was upon an occasion and under circumstances which have created general alarm and terror.

We are unable to protect ourselves without aid, and therefore pray for the protection of the United States forces.

> HENRY E. COOPER,
> F. W. MCCHESNEY,
> W. C. WILDER,
> C. BOLTE,
> A. BROWN,
> WILLIAM O. SMITH,
> HENRY WATERHOUSE,
> THEO. F. LANSING,
> ED. SUHR,
> L. A. THURSTON,
> JOHN EMMELUTH,
> WM. R. CASTLE,
> S. A. MCCANDLESS,
> *Citizens' Committee of Safety.*

Of the signers of this letter five were American citizens. Nothing could be more significant than this attempt testified to by Mr. Smith, to prevent the landing of the troops on Monday evening. If there was danger of riot and disturbance, if general alarm and terror prevailed, if there was pressing need of the United States' assistance, why did this committee wish to deprive themselves of the surest means of safety? How is it possible to explain their action in this regard upon the supposition that the alarm and terror which they speak of really existed? What explanation could they give to the citizens whose "wives and families were helpless and in terror of an expected uprising of the mob," if any such there were?

But it may be asked what harm could the committee have anticipated from the landing of the troops? Mr. Smith answers the question plainly enough. The mass meeting broke up sooner than the committee expected; they did not know what to do. They were not in readiness to take the final steps just yet: plans were not perfected, papers not drawn, and the coming of the troops might possibly have brought about a state of things which they could not anticipate, and for which they might not be prepared. So they went straight to the American minister, with whom they had left their written request, ready to be complied with when they said the word, but found that he had already acted and they were too late.

Mr. John A. McCandless, a member of the Committee of Safety and of the Provisional Government, in his testimony before the committee, goes into this matter a little more fully:[16]

Senator GRAY. — Was anything said in your meeting on Saturday, after your Committee of Safety was formed and you had cleared the room, about Mr. Stevens and the United States ship "Boston"?
Mr. McCANDLESS. — Yes; we talked that over.
Senator GRAY. — So soon as your committee was formed?
Mr. McCANDLESS. — Well, it was during the conversation.
The CHAIRMAN. — On Saturday?
Senator GRAY. — Yes. Was anything said about the attitude of Mr. Stevens?

Mr. McCandless. — It was talked of — what his attitude would be.

Senator Gray. — Was anybody deputed to go and see him?

Mr. McCandless. — Yes; I think there was a committee of one or two appointed on Saturday afternoon to have a talk with him, to ascertain what his attitude would be in the then crisis.

Senator Gray. — Did that committee report?

Mr. McCandless. — The report was that there was no information; that he was entirely non-committal.

Senator Gray. — Who said that?

Mr. McCandless. — Mr. Thurston, I believe.

Senator Gray. — But said he would protect life and property?

Mr. McCandless. — Yes.

Senator Gray. — He did not say he was non-committal?

Mr. McCandless. — Well, he was non-committal as to contending forces, but would protect life and property.

Senator Gray. — Was anything said by them that conveyed the idea to you that Mr. Stevens was hostile or indifferent to the movement of the Committee of Safety, or was without sympathy for it?

Mr. McCandless. — I think not.

Senator Gray. — Anything at all?

Mr. McCandless. — I think we felt this way, that without any encouragement from him we certainly had the sympathy of the American minister.

Senator Gray. — That was the general feeling, was it not?

Mr. McCandless. — Yes.

Senator Frye. — A committee was sent to Minister Stevens to request him not to land the troops then?

Mr. McCandless. — Yes; we did not feel certain that night, and thought we would get our strength better in a day or two.

Senator Gray. — That the landing of the troops might bring on a crisis?

Mr. McCandless. — Yes.

Senator Gray. — If you were not as well prepared as you thought you would be later?

Mr. McCandless. — No, sir.

. . . .

Senator Gray. — Had Minister Stevens been advised of the project for a Provisional Government and annexation to the United States?

Mr. McCandless. — I do not know.

Senator Gray. — Do you know whether it was understood there that he knew what was going on?

THE HAWAIIAN INCIDENT 25

Mr. McCandless. — Well, everybody knew it.

Senator Gray. — Did you not understand that he knew it — was not that your opinion ?

Mr. McCandless. — It would be my opinion that he would know.

Senator Gray. — Do you not know, and did you not know then, that he did understand it ?

Mr. McCandless. — No ; I do not know it.

Senator Gray. — It was not talked about ?

Mr. McCandless. — Oh, it was discussed, certainly.

Senator Gray. — In what respect was it discussed ?

Mr. McCandless. — It was discussed in respect to what would be the attitude of the American minister.

Senator Gray. — Was it thought his attitude would be sympathetic or unsympathetic ?

Mr. McCandless. — There were doubts about that.

Senator Gray. — Were there any doubts that Mr. Stevens sympathized with the movement ?

Mr. McCandless. — Yes.

Senator Gray. — Did you doubt it ?

Mr. McCandless. — It was doubted that much that we requested him, after we requested the troops to be landed, not to have them landed, for fear it would precipitate a crisis.

Senator Gray. — Had you any doubt at that time in regard to Mr. Stevens's sympathies with this movement ?

Mr. McCandless. — I do not think there was any serious doubt in my mind about it, although I was one of the members who took the side that we would stand a better show on Monday afternoon not to have the troops landed.

Senator Gray. — When did you want them landed ?

Mr. McCandless. — Well, I thought they had better be let alone. The idea prevailed that they had better be let alone, and when the crisis came he would land them himself.

Senator Gray. — Then it was your idea it would be better not to have them landed ? I see it stated here that the proposition of the committee was that they should be landed the next morning at 9 or 10 o'clock. When did you think they should be landed ?

Mr. McCandless. — I do not think there was a time stated. We thought it was better to let them stay there because the crisis would be precipitated.

Senator Daniel. — What were you afraid of in that crisis ?

Mr. McCandless. — The Queen's forces.

Senator Daniel. — That they would suppress the revolution ?

Mr. McCandless. — Yes ; might attempt it.

Senator DANIEL. — Do you think they could do it?
Mr. MCCANDLESS. — I do not think so.
Senator DANIEL. — Did you then think so?
Mr. MCCANDLESS. — We did not think so Monday morning.

The idea prevailed that the troops had better be left alone, and that when the crisis came he would land them himself! What language could better express the confidence which the committee felt in the friendly zeal of the American minister; or better show the real opinion of the committee as to the probability of an uprising of the mob?

The following is an abstract from a statement made for the Congressional Committee by Mr. W. C. Wilder:[17]

For ten days prior to noon of Saturday, January 14, the day that the Queen attempted her revolutionary act, the United States steamship "Boston," with Minister Stevens on board, had not been in port. There had been no revolutionary meetings or conferences; such a thing had not been thought of. There had not been any consultation with Minister Stevens with regard to the matter, though of course he must have seen what a perilous condition the country was getting into. There were several meetings at the office of W. O. Smith that day, after the attempted promulgation of the new constitution. I was not present at the first impromptu gathering; at that meeting I was named as one of the Committee of Safety. A telephonic message was sent to me to meet the committee that evening, and again we met at his office. The only business done besides talking over matters was the appointment of the committee to canvass and report what arms and ammunition and how many men could be secured.

Another committee was appointed, of which I was a member, to call upon Minister-resident John L. Stevens to discuss the situation. We went at once and talked over the whole matter, and we asked what his course would be should we take possession of the Government and declare a Provisional Government. Mr. Stevens replied that if we obtained possession of the Government building and the archives, and established a Government, and became, in fact, the Government, he should of course recognize us. The matter of landing the troops from the "Boston" was not mentioned at that meeting.

The United States troops came duly to hand at about

5 o'clock Monday afternoon. Lieut. Lucien Young, of the "Boston," tells of the landing and the subsequent march.

After speaking of drills on shore, he says:[18]

> We had one of the best battalions I have ever seen.
>
> The CHAIRMAN. — What is the strength?
>
> A. Three companies of blue jackets; one of artillery and one of marines, making one hundred and fifty-four all told, and about ten officers.
>
> Senator BUTLER. — How many marines?
>
> A. Thirty-two, I think.
>
> The CHAIRMAN. — What time did you leave the ship?
>
> A. About 5 o'clock — I suppose about quarter of 5. We were ordered to land at 4, and our battalion was gotten together immediately after dinner, which was between 12 and 1. That was Monday, the 16th.
>
> The CHAIRMAN. — I want to know if any troops left the ship before the detachment which you commanded.
>
> Mr. YOUNG. — No; we landed in a body.
>
> The CHAIRMAN. — You went first?
>
> Mr. YOUNG. — Yes.
>
> The CHAIRMAN. — That was 5 o'clock in the evening?
>
> Mr. YOUNG. — Five o'clock in the evening. We got the men armed and equipped for heavy marching order — knapsacks and double belts of cartridges holding from 60 to 80 rounds. And I had the caisson filled, taking in all about 14,000 rounds of calibre .45 for the rifle and Gatling, 1,200 rounds of calibre .38 for the revolvers, and 174 common explosive shells for the revolving cannon. Each one of these belts carried from 60 to 80 rounds. About 3 o'clock Minister Stevens came on board and was in consultation with Captain Wiltse.
>
> Q. Where was the company ordered to go?
>
> A. We had no definite point at all. We landed at Brewer's wharf and marched up to the corner of Fort and Merchant streets, where the Consul-general's office was, and there left a marine company which was to protect the American Legation and Consulate. The rest of the battalion turned and marched down King street in front of the Palace, and as we passed the Palace the Queen was standing on the balcony, when we gave her the royal salute by drooping the colors and four ruffles on the drums. We passed the Palace two hundred and fifty yards, and there waited until we could find some place to go into camp. We made an effort at first to get the old armory near the landing, so as to be near our base of supplies and throw out

pickets in case of emergency. But we failed to get that, and then tried to get the Opera House. They were the only two buildings near the centre of the town, and not being able to get them we went to the yard of a white man named Atherton, and there we bivouacked under the trees in the rain until 9.30 P.M., when the aid to Captain Wiltse reported they had secured a little hall in the rear of the Opera House, known as Arion Hall, which is used as a Mormon temple now, I believe. We marched there and went into camp.

Thus the United States troops are settled for the night.

In the meantime, on Monday, a protest had been made against the landing of the troops by the governor of Oahu, the island on which Honolulu is situated, as follows: [19]

OFFICE GOVERNOR OF OAHU,
HONOLULU, Jan. 16, 1893.

SIR: It is my duty to solemnly protest to your Excellency against the landing this evening, without permission from the proper authorities, of an armed force from the United States ship "Boston." Your Excellency well knows that when you have desired to land naval forces of the United States for the purpose of drill, permission by the local authorities has been readily accorded. On the present occasion, however, the circumstances are different, and ostensibly the present landing is for the discharge of functions which are distinctly responsible duties of the Hawaiian Government. Such being the case, I am compelled to impress upon your Excellency the international questions involved in the matter and the grave responsibility thereby assumed.

While solemnly protesting to your Excellency against this unwarrantable proceeding to which I have referred,

I have the honor to remain, Sir,
    Your Excellency's obedient and humble servant,
                    A. S. CLEGHORN,
                        Governor of Oahu.

His Excellency JOHN L. STEVENS,
   Envoy Extraordinary and Minister Plenipotentiary, United States of America.

To which Mr. Stevens makes the following reply the next day, Tuesday: [20]

UNITED STATES LEGATION,
HONOLULU, Jan. 17, 1893.

SIR: Yours of yesterday, the 16th, regarding the landing of the United States naval forces in Honolulu, is received. I have carefully read its terms and import. My responsibility as the United States minister plenipotentiary at this critical time in Hawaiian affairs it is impossible for me to ignore. I assure you that in whatever responsibility the American diplomatic and naval representatives have assumed or may assume, we shall do our utmost to regard the welfare of all present and interests concerned.

Yours sincerely, and with the kindest consideration,

JOHN L. STEVENS.

Hon. A. S. CLEGHORN,
Governor of Oahu.

This landing of troops upon a foreign shore not only without permission, but even against the protest of the authorities, and in defiance of a Queen who was recognized as such by these very troops themselves, was a deliberate and flagrant act of war, unless justified by an actual necessity for the protection of American life and property, and carried out with perfect sincerity and good faith. Perhaps nothing could show Mr. Stevens's utter contempt for the Hawaiian Government more clearly than his neglect to give Governor Cleghorn the slightest intimation as to his purpose or motives in taking so extreme action upon the governor's own soil.

Of course all parties concerned in this landing of the troops have felt the necessity of dwelling upon and magnifying in every way the need of protection to "life and property," and it may be well in this connection to call attention to a very significant fact. At the time now spoken of there were in Hawaii representatives of England, Germany, Austro-Hungary, Italy, Russia, Spain, The Netherlands, Denmark, Belgium, Mexico, Chili, Peru, and China. It might be fairly presumed that these gentlemen would be solicitous for the protection of " life and property." Yet while Mr. Stevens is supposed to have been in a state of the most nervous anxiety about danger to life and property, there is nothing in the whole course of the 2,200 pages of the committee's Report, in all the voluminous examinations and interviews, which shows, or in any manner indicates, that any of these ministerial or consular officers felt any anxiety, or were otherwise than perfectly tranquil during the four days of the revolution.[1] That the English minister was disposed to look at the whole matter in a somewhat humorous light will appear hereafter.

It is seen that the troops marched through the streets of Honolulu, passed the Palace, and went to the United States Legation and Consulate; for the protection of both these places, — where American citizens would be likely to seek refuge in case of a riot or hostile demonstrations, — a company of marines, thirty-five in number, was thought sufficient. The remainder of the forces then marched to the land of one Atherton and finally to Arion Hall. Why was this place chosen? Arion Hall is a building lying in the rear of the Opera House, so-called, which is south of the Palace grounds and about two hundred yards distant from the Palace. It is west of the Government building, and is separated from it only by a narrow street. The question asked above is answered by Mr. Stevens: [21]

Senator FRYE. — As a matter of fact, is Arion Hall, so far as American property is concerned, — and I mean by that, of course, residences as well as anything else, — a reasonably central location?

Mr. STEVENS. — A reasonably central location.

Senator FRYE. — Do you know of any place large enough, other than that, for quartering those troops in the city of Honolulu?

Mr. STEVENS. — Not obtainable. I had thought of another on my own street. If Arion Hall had not been gotten we

---

[1] With the exception of H. F. Glade, German consul and Austro-Hungarian consul, who took part in the mass meeting.

would have tried another hall, which was nearer me, but the owner was not there.

Senator FRYE. — The only purpose you had was to place the troops where they could be protected during the night?

Mr. STEVENS. — Yes; and where they would be useful in case of fire.

Lieut. De Witt Coffman, commanding a company in the battalion of troops landed, testifies as follows: [22]

Senator GRAY. — Was there, to your knowledge, any other building suitable for the use of the troops of the "Boston" than the Opera House and Arion Hall?

Mr. COFFMAN. — Yes.

Senator GRAY. — Where?

Mr. COFFMAN. — On Nuuana avenue, a little more than half-way between the United States Consulate and the American minister's residence.

Senator GRAY. — What sort of building was that?

Mr. COFFMAN. — It was a large, three-story brand-new hotel, and unoccupied.

Senator GRAY. — Do you know who owned it?

Mr. COFFMAN. — Mr. John Thomas Waterhouse, who was present while our troops were standing in the street waiting to find out where Mr. Atherton's was.

Senator GRAY. — Do you know whether that building was obtainable?

Mr. COFFMAN. — I have no doubt in the world that it was obtainable.

Senator GRAY. — Is that simply an opinion?

Mr. COFFMAN. — That is my opinion.

Senator GRAY. — Did you hear Mr. Waterhouse say anything about it?

Mr. COFFMAN. — I heard Mr. Waterhouse say that he was glad to see the troops, and marched down in front of us after we had halted. He said, "I am glad to see this," and passed on in front of our troops, as much as to say he was glad to see our troops.

Senator GRAY. — He owned that hotel building?

Mr. COFFMAN. — Yes.

Senator GRAY. — Is the situation of that building in a more thickly built up part of the town?

Mr. COFFMAN. — I cannot say more thickly built up; but there are fine residences around there, and it is more accessible to the business portion.

Senator GRAY. — Was it nearer to what you considered the property of American citizens than Arion Hall?
Mr. COFFMAN. — Yes.
Senator GRAY. — More so, or how?
Mr. COFFMAN. — It was nearer to the residence portion, which was the part which would be attacked in any incendiary work to go on.
Senator GRAY. — Will you point on that map where it is?
Mr. COFFMAN. — On Nuuana avenue.
Senator GRAY. — You say it is on Nuuana avenue, a little more than half-way between the United States Consulate and the United States Legation?
Mr. COFFMAN. — Yes. (Indicating on diagram.) There is Nuuana avenue; that is the Legation; it is about here — the house is not down here.
Senator GRAY. — It was a new and unoccupied building?
Mr. COFFMAN. — It was a new and unoccupied building.
Senator GRAY. — Large enough to have accommodated your force?
Mr. COFFMAN. — Yes.
Senator GRAY. — Did any one suggest the use of that building?
Mr. COFFMAN. — Yes; I did myself.
Senator GRAY. — Where and when?
Mr. COFFMAN. — When the troops were drawn up — I think first when they were drawn up in the street, and certainly afterward, when we were waiting for a place to go.
Senator GRAY. — Whom did you suggest it to?
Mr. COFFMAN. — To the officers in general.

About the 27th of February, 1893, Admiral Skerrett, of the United States Navy, arrived at Honolulu in the United States flagship "Mohican." He looked over Arion Hall and its position relative to the other buildings, and made the following report: [23]

ADMIRAL SKERRETT TO MR. BLOUNT.
U.S.S. "BOSTON," FLAGSHIP OF THE PACIFIC STATION,
HONOLULU, HAWAIIAN ISLANDS. May 20, 1893.

SIR: I have examined with a view of inspection the premises first occupied by the force landed from the U.S.S. "Boston," and known as Arion Hall, situated on the west side of the Government building. The position of this location is in the rear of a large brick building

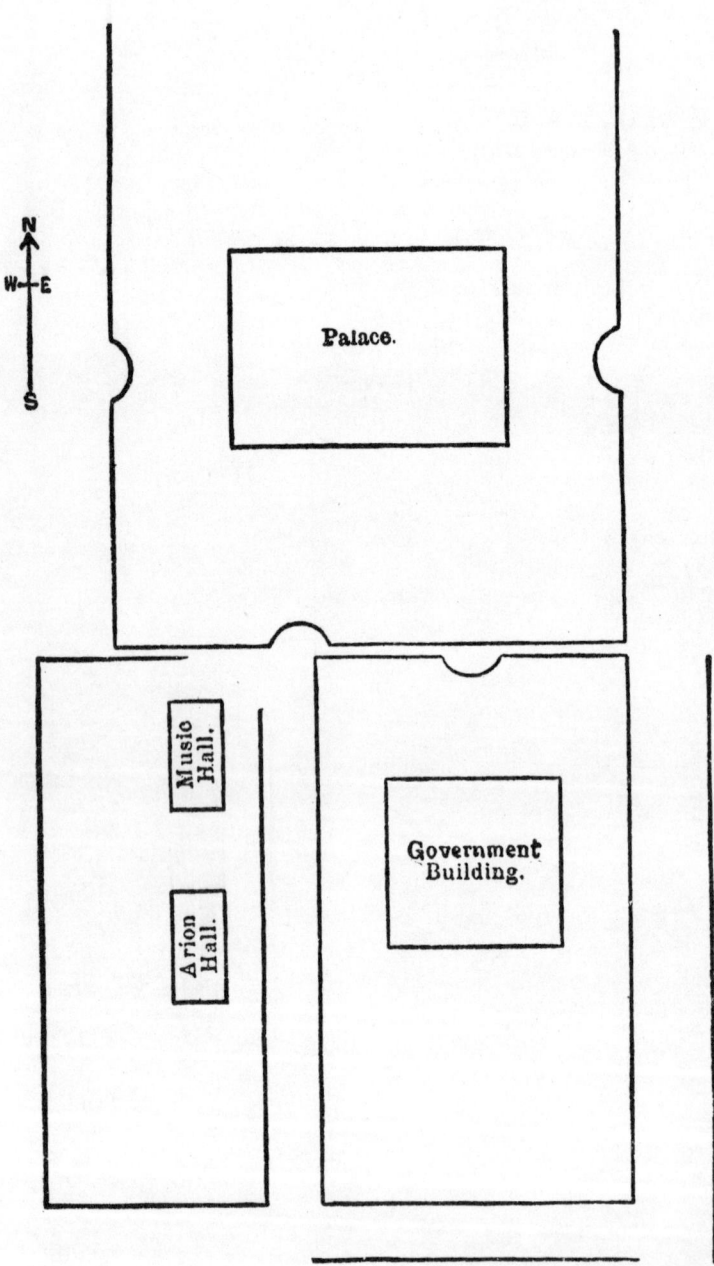

known as Music Hall. The street it faces is comparatively a narrow one, the building itself facing the Government building. In my opinion it was unadvisable to locate the troops there if they were landed for the protection of the United States citizens, being distantly removed from the business portion of the town and generally far away from the United States Legation and Consulate-general, as well as being distant from the houses and residences of United States citizens. It will be seen from the accompanying sketch that had the Provisional Government troops been attacked from the east, such attack would have placed them in the line of fire.

Had Music Hall been seized by the Queen's troops, they would have been under their fire, had such been their desire. It is for these reasons that I consider the position occupied as illy selected. Naturally, if they were landed with a view to support the Provisional Government troops then occupying the Government building, it was a wise choice, as they could enfilade any troops attacking them from the Palace grounds in front. There is nothing further for me to state with reference to this matter, and as has been called by you to my attention; — all of which is submitted for your consideration.

Very respectfully,

J. S. SKERRETT,
Rear-Admiral U.S. Navy, Commanding U.S. Naval Force,
Pacific Station.

Col. J. H. BLOUNT,
U.S. Minister Plenipotentiary and Envoy Extraordinary,
Honolulu, Hawaiian Islands.

The sketch accompanying this letter is here reproduced.

Before taking up the events of the fourth day (Tuesday) it may be well to go back to the mass meeting held on Monday. The number of those present has been variously given by those sympathizing with the revolution, but perhaps a fair average of their estimate would be 1,200 to 1,300 persons.[1] Seven speeches were made, of which we have

---

[1] Mr. Stevens says over 1,300; Mr. McCandless, 1,000 to 1,200; the "Hawaiian Gazette," a paper strongly in favor of Provisional Government, says 1,260 by actual count, while many others came later; Francis R. Day, a sympathizer with the revolutionists, 1,200 to 1,300.

In a statement made by Mr. Thurston for publication, at Washington, Nov. 21,

room only for the close of the first, that of Mr. Thurston, and of the last, that of Mr. R. G. Greene.[25]

It is an old saying that a royal promise is made to be broken. Fellow-citizens remember it. We have not sought this situation. Last Saturday the sun rose on a peaceful and smiling city; to-day it is otherwise. Whose fault is it — Queen Liliuokalani's? It is not her fault that the streets have not run red with blood. She has printed a proclamation expressing her repentance for what she has done, and at the same time — perhaps sent out by the same carriers — her organ prints an extra with her speech, with bitterer language than that quoted in the "Advertiser." She wants us to sleep on a slumbering volcano, which will some morning spew out blood and destroy us all. The constitution gives us the right to assemble peacefully and express our grievances. We are here doing that to-day without arms. The man who has not the spirit to rise after the menace to our liberties, has no right to keep them. Has the tropic sun cooled and thinned our blood, or have we flowing in our veins the warm, rich blood which makes men love liberty and die for it? I move the adoption of the resolution. [Tumultuous applause!]

Mr. Greene said:

We all agree about the case. The question is the remedy. John Greene, of Rhode Island, entered the War of the Revolution and served throughout. His son, my father, served through the War of 1812, until that little matter was settled. In 1862 John Greene, my father, stood before a meeting like this, and said he had four sons in the war, of whom I was the youngest, and would serve himself if he was not too old. This experience has biased my judgment as to some matters of civil government. It is too late to throw obstacles across the path of its progress here. I have adopted this flag and am loyal to it, but I am not willing to go one step back in the matter of

---

1893, setting forth the position and claims of the Hawaiian Government, and making reply to charges contained in Mr. Blount's report, appears the following: "At 2 o'clock on the afternoon of Monday, the 16th, a mass meeting of 3,000 unarmed men was held within a block of the Palace. The meeting was addressed by a number of speakers, all denouncing the Queen."[24]

Seeing that all the right which Mr. Thurston and his friends had to give away the Hawaiian Islands, with their 90,000 people, purported to be derived from the action of this meeting, this slight exaggeration of the numbers present may be looked upon with charity.

civil liberty, and I will give the last drop of Rhode Island blood in my veins to go forward and not back. [Cheers.]

Chairman Wilder read the latter part of the resolution.

It was passed by a unanimous standing vote, without a dissenting voice and amid tremendous cheers, after which the meeting broke up.

After reading these remarks, thus received with tumultuous applause, the reader will hardly be prepared for the outcome of the meeting, which was extremely mild, and partaking somewhat of the nature of an anti-climax. The final resolution is here given:

6. And whereas such committee has recommended the calling of this mass meeting of citizens to protest against and condemn such action, and has this day presented a report to such meeting, denouncing the action of the Queen and her supporters as being unlawful, unwarranted, in derogation of the rights of the people, endangering the peace of the community, and tending to excite riot, and cause the loss of life and destruction of property;

Now, therefore, we, the citizens of Honolulu, of all nationalities, and regardless of political party affiliations, do hereby condemn and denounce the action of the Queen and her supporters;

And we do hereby ratify the appointment and indorse the action taken and report made by the said Committee of Safety; and we do hereby further empower such committee to further consider the situation and further devise such ways and means as may be necessary to secure the permanent maintenance of law and order, and the protection of life, liberty, and property in Hawaii.

Not a word here about dethroning the Queen or taking possession of the Government building, nor of handing over the islands to the United States, nor can such word be found in any of the seven speeches. But whatever may have been the character of this assemblage, whatever may be thought of its action, and whatever were the rights and powers which it assumed to grant, they are all contained in that resolution; and upon the strength of it the committee proceeded that very Monday night, nearly twenty-four hours before the surrender of the Queen, to charter the steamer "Claudine," wherein "Commissioners" embarked on Friday, the 20th, for the United States, with a treaty of annexation in their pockets.

Mr. Bolte, in the following extract from his statement to Mr. Blount, gives us the reason for the excessive caution of the managers of the mass meeting; they did not know whether their action would be indorsed; a fact pretty effectually disposing of the theory that there was a grand uprising of the people, desperately bent on protecting their rights and liberties from the assaults of tyranny; and showing that this little band of revolutionists were never sure of their ground, but felt their way gradually along, always reaching out for aid from the United States and the United States minister and the United States troops. He also incidentally affords us some information about the station-house.[1] He says:[26]

This committee met several times at various places, and decided that the only perfect safeguard against future occurrences of this kind would lie in annexation to the United States, or in a protectorate, or in anything of that kind, but that we could not go on with the form of government as it was then. They decided to call a mass meeting of citizens on Monday afternoon at 2 o'clock, and see what people there would say about it. At this meeting were various speakers, some of the committee of thirteen, and also others. The people were asked by the speakers if they were satisfied with the promises the Queen had made, and let the matter drop, let everything go on as it was before, or if they wanted a change and guarantees for

---

[1] There is considerable discrepancy in the evidence as to the number of men at the station-house, but we may take the number as stated by the Commissioners, Mr. Thurston and others, in their letter of Feb. 3, 1893, to Mr. Foster:[27] "On the afternoon of the same day, the Queen then having about four hundred men under arms, and the people being in open preparation for dethroning her, with every indication of a conflict, the United States troops landed, and a guard was stationed at the American Consulate and Legation, and the remainder were quartered in a public hall hired for that purpose."

the future. They desired guarantees for the future, and appointed the committee of thirteen — or rather continued the committee — to take such farther steps as might be necessary.

Q. Let me ask you what you meant and what people meant by saying they wanted guarantees?

A. I meant a change of government. What the people meant I cannot say, but I am fully convinced that they meant the same as it has been very often spoken of during the last few years.

Q. What has been spoken of so often?

A. Annexation to the United States has been advocated publicly in the papers — I meant change of government.

Q. Why didn't you use language that conveyed distinctly the idea — dethronement of the Queen, and annexation to the United States?

A. The Hawaiian Government, as it was then, was still in existence, and in stating there publicly we wanted to dethrone the Queen and have a government of our own, with an intention of being annexed to the United States, might be going a little too far.

Q. You mean making you liable to interference on the part of the local authorities?

A. Yes.

Q. And that you were trying to avoid at that time?

A. Yes, especially for this reason. We did not know whether the action of the committee would be indorsed by this large majority of the people at the mass meeting. We thought it would.

Q. Was there any expression in that meeting asking for guarantees for the future in the shape of a vote?

A. Yes; the resolution was all prepared.

Q. It was a resolution indorsing the report of the Committee of Safety?

A. Yes. The meeting dispersed, and the Committee of Safety went back to W. O. Smith's office to talk matters over.

Q. What time in the day was that?

A. About half-past 3. After talking matters over, and seeing that the Queen had concentrated her forces, — meaning thereby that the soldiers were all in the barracks, — the Palace barricaded with sand-bags, and the station-house barricaded —

Q. How about the Government house?

A. I didn't notice anything going on there. The station-house has always been considered the stronghold of the Government. It looked as if there might be trouble. So we came to the conclusion to ask Mr. Stevens if he would protect the life and property of the citizens by sending some soldiers ashore, stating that we considered the situation very grave — even dangerous. After a short while Mr. Stevens sent his answer that he would.

Q. Sent it to the meeting?

A. Yes; sent it to the meeting, and then at 5 o'clock the soldiers came ashore. They were quartered at various places. That same evening, Monday, January 16, the Committee of Safety had another meeting.

Let us now take up the events of the fourth day, Tuesday, the 17th. Mr. W. O. Smith has informed us that a meeting of the Committee of Safety was held at 10 o'clock in the forenoon, at which he says Mr. Dole signed his written resignation as a judge of the Supreme Court, and forwarded it to the Minister of Foreign Affairs.

The meeting adjourned and met again at 1.30. After some mention in regard to the choice of members, Mr. Smith says:[28]

The members of the Executive Council and Advisory Committee were then finally approved and acted upon.

The committee of thirteen then signed the proclamation, and the Executive Council then signed the commission of J. H. Soper as commander-in-chief of the forces, and three copies of the proclamation were completed. The final signing of the papers was completed about twenty minutes past 2, and after a little delay the committee of thirteen, with the Executive and Advisory Councils, started to proceed to the Government building. They had hardly reached the corner of Merchant street before a shot was heard, and it was reported that a policeman had been shot at E. O. Hall & Sons' store, and people were seen running from the direction of the Government building towards the spot, and there was considerable commotion. The committee and councils proceeded to the Government building and the proclamation was read. Previous to starting, leaving my office, Mr. Dole requested Mr. A. S. Wilcox to go up to the Government building, and come back and report whether there was any armed force at the Government building. He went up and looked through, and went through to Queen street, and came back and reported that he did not see any armed men.

Mr. S. M. Damon is a man who played a very prominent part at the close of the proceedings in question, having been the one, as will be seen, who finally brought about the surrender of the Queen. He was not a member of the original Committee of Safety, but at the time referred to was a member of the Provisional Government. He is vouched for by Mr. Stevens as follows: [29]

>   Senator GRAY. — What sort of a person is Mr. Damon?
>   Mr. STEVENS. — He is a man of the highest respectability.
>   Senator GRAY. — What is his business?
>   Mr. STEVENS. — He is a banker. Mr. Damon is the son of an American missionary, who went there forty years ago, and whom our Government recognized officially. He became a clerk to Banker Bishop and a great friend of the natives. He is an excellent financial manager, and largely increased the value of the property of two prominent natives. When the natives get into any financial trouble Damon is the man they go to to get them out. He is a man of the highest character.

Mr. Damon's testimony was given at great length and is of great importance, and it is ventured to give it here in full, with the exception of a portion towards the close, where he answers some inquiries as to the form of government desired by the natives, etc., not bearing upon the question now under consideration.[30]

HONOLULU, April 29, 1893.

Mr. BLOUNT. — How long have you lived here?
Mr. DAMON. — I was born here in 1845. I have been away several times — perhaps to the extent of three or four years in that time.
Q. Where were you on the 14th of January, 1893, at the time the proclamation dethroning the Queen and establishing the Provisional Government was read?
A. I was at Honolulu. I was one of the members of that body who went up.
Q. The paper was read by Mr. Cooper?
A. By Judge Cooper.
Q. How many of you were there in that body which went up — about?
A. The whole body. There would be four of the Executive and fourteen of the Advisory

Q. Please look at this paper and see if they are the persons.
A. Thurston was not present, and I do not think Wilhelm was there.
Q. Where did you start from?
A. From W. O. Smith's office on Fort street.
Q. And what street did you take going from there?
A. We walked up directly to the Government house on Merchant street. It was suggested that a part should go by the way of Queen street, but a majority of us went by way of Merchant street.
Q. What was the idea for dividing the committee?
A. So that it should not attract so much attention, and it would be safer perhaps to have it divided than going in mass.
Q. Was it because it occurred to them that it might invite attack if they went in mass?
A. That was partly the idea — that it was more prudent. I think we, most of us, walked together — not compactly, but together.
Q. Any crowd following you?
A. No; the crowd was attracted to the corner of Fort and King streets, owing to the shot that was fired by Mr. Good at a policeman. In fact, the crowd cleared from the Government house and was attracted there. From all directions they centred at the corner of Hall's store.
Q. You found, then, scarcely any one at the Government house when the committee arrived?
A. Scarcely any one there except porters. After Mr. Cooper began to read the proclamation, then different ones came out of the offices — clerks and officials — while the proclamation was being read.
Q. Some of the Provisional Government troops, or rather troops raised at the direction of the Committee of Safety, came on the ground before the reading of the proclamation was finished?
A. When we arrived there was but one man with a rifle on the premises — Mr. Oscar White; but some little time later they commenced to come in from the armory, troops that were under the supervision of Colonel Soper.
Q. Was that before or during the reading of the proclamation?
A. During the reading. Toward the end of it.
Q. How many troops came in? Do you have any knowledge of the number you have enlisted?
A. There were enough came in to make us feel more decidedly at ease than before they arrived.

Q. You could not say how many there were?
A. No; they kept coming in right along. They got to be quite a body.
Q. After the reading of the proclamation the late ministers were sent for?
A. After the reading of the proclamation we adjourned to the office of the Minister of the Interior, and then we commenced to formulate our plans and get ourselves into working order. Mr. Dole was at the head. While we were there in consultation, Mr. Cornwell and Mr. Parker came up there from the station-house and held a conference with us.
Q. What was the purport of that conference?
A. The result of that conference was that Mr. Bolte and myself were requested to return with Mr. Cornwell and Mr. Parker to the station-house and recommend and urge upon the parties in power at the police-station to surrender to the Provisional Government. We had a conference with the ministers in the room occupied generally by the Deputy Marshal. There were present Messrs. Peterson, Colburn, Parker, Cornwell, Bolte, and later Mr. Neumann, who was asked to come in. After consultation of the matter of their yielding up their power to the Provisional Government they asked to be let alone for a few moments, and I went into one of the rear cells in the corridor with Marshal Wilson and urged him very strongly to give up any hope or any thought of making any attack — or resistance, more properly.
Q. What reason did you give him?
A. I cannot remember at the present moment giving him a reason, but I remember distinctly saying to him: "Now, if you will coöperate with us, if in future I can be of service to you I will do so."
Q. Was there any suggestion of sympathy on the part of the United States minister in your movement?
A. While I was in the station-house a man by the name of Bowler said to me: "We are all prepared, but I will never fight against the American flag."
Q. Was there anything in the conversation between you and him, in which any intimation direct or indirect that the United States minister was in sympathy with you or the United States troops and officers?
A. I cannot remember any definite thing, but from Mr. Bowler's remark they must have thought that the United States troops were here for some purpose.
Q. Was Mr. Bowler with the Queen's party?
A. He was. He was part of the force in the station-house.

Q. Did you say anything at all indicating an opinion that there was any sympathy on the part of Mr. Stevens or Captain Wiltse with the movement for the new Government?
A. I cannot remember. I may possibly have said so.
Q. Did you think so at that time?
A. I may have had an impression, but I know nothing about it.
Q. What was your impression?
A. My impression was, seeing the troops landed here in this time of excitement and turmoil, that — well, I suppose I might say that they could not stand it any longer, the Americans could not stand it any longer.
Q. Your impression, then, was that the American minister and Captain Wiltse and the troops were in sympathy with the movement of the white residents here in the pending controversy between them and the Queen?
A. While we were in the Government building and during the reading of the proclamation and while we were all extremely nervous as to our personal safety, I asked one of the men with me there: "Will not the American troops support us?" Finally I asked one of the men to go over and ask Lieutenant Swinburne if he was not going to send some one over to protect us. The man returned and said to me, "Captain Wiltse's orders are, 'I remain passive.'" That is all I know of what passed between us.
Q. You speak of your impression. That relates to a particular conversation between two or three persons; but what was your impression as to the matter of whether or not the American minister and the American naval officers were in sympathy with the movement?
A. I was perfectly nonplussed by not receiving any support. I could not imagine why we were there without being supported by American troops, prior to the troops coming from the armory. We were not supported in any way.
Q. You had not been in council with the Committee of Public Safety up to that time?
A. No.
Q. Well, the troops were — how far off from the reading of the proclamation?
A. They were over in that yard known as Gilson yard in the rear of the Music Hall. They were quartered there.
Q. Any artillery?
A. I think they had a small gun — Gatling gun and howitzer.

Q. Where were they pointed — in what direction?
A. I cannot tell you.
Q. You were surprised that they did not come into the grounds while the proclamation was being read. Is that what you mean by not supporting you?
A. I had no definite information what the movement was, as I told you before in a private interview, but knowing that they were on shore I supposed that they would support us, and when they did not support us, and we were there for fifteen or twenty minutes, I was perfectly astonished that we were in that position without any support.
Q. How far would you say, in yards, it was from where the proclamation was being read to where the nearest troops were?
A. I think about seventy-five yards.
Q. Was there a piece of artillery in the street between the building the troops were stationed in and the Government building?
A. The only piece of firearms of any kind in that street was Oscar White's rifle. We met him as we came around the corner.
Q. Did you have occasion to look there to see?
A. We stopped before turning into the side gate to converse with Oscar White, before proceeding into the Government building.
Q. Are you sure there was not a piece of artillery in that street before the reading of the proclamation?
A. I cannot tell you; but the only gun I could see was Oscar White's. I remarked, "Oscar, this is not so very prudent for you to be here with only one rifle in this street."
Q. Where did you see the troops first?
A. I came up from Monolalua by a back street and turned into Nuuana street, one house above Mr. Stevens's, and as I turned the corner I saw the American troops marching up towards Mr. Stevens's house, and directly in front of his house.
Q. Did you meet Mr. Henry Waterhouse?
A. I met him there at that time.
Q. What conversation passed between you?
A. I think I said, "Henry, what does all this mean?" If I remember rightly now, he said, "It is all up."
Q. And what did you understand by the expression, "It is all up"?
A. I understand from that that the American troops had taken possession of the island. That was my impression.

Q. And was that favorable to the Queen or favorable to the other side, as you understood it?
A. That was distinctly favorable to the foreign element here.
Q. You mean the movement for a Provisional Government?
A. Yes.
Q. Did you see Mr. Stevens that day?
A. No; I did not see him that day.
Q. What is Mr. Waterhouse doing now?
A. Henry? He is a member of the Council.
Q. Was he a member of the Committee of Public Safety?
A. If I remember right, he was.
Q. Is that his signature? (Exhibiting letter of Committee of Public Safety to Mr. Stevens.)
A. Yes, it is.
Q. Did he seem then pleased or alarmed?
A. He was very much strained and excited. There was no pleasure in it, but still there was a feeling of security. That was it. He evinced a feeling of security. He was not smiling or joking.
Q. It was not a joking time. Well, you say there was nothing in the first visit of yours to the station-house to indicate any impression on your part that you believed the United States minister or the United States troops, or both, were in sympathy with the movement of the Committee of Safety?
A. I was nonplussed. I did suppose they were going to support us.
Q. You did not say anything to the people in the station-house to lead them to suppose you were hopeful of aid?
A. I cannot remember saying it now; I might have done so.
Q. Did you say it at any place?
A. I do not remember; I may have said it.
Q. Was there an effort on the part of those who were moving for a change of government to make that impression?
A. I think there was.
Q. Was that impression among the whites generally?
A. That I cannot say. I know there was that impression. Some of the members tried to convey that impression.
Q. On what occasion?
A. Many occasions. One particular occasion was while we were in the Government building, the day the proclamation was read.
Q. What was said, and who said it?

A. Charles Carter said to me, "After you are in possession of the Government building, the troops will support you." I think that was his remark.

Q. Was he on the Committee of Public Safety?

A. I think so.

Q. Was he in the party that went up to read the proclamation?

A. He was present there during the time it was read. Whether he went up with us or not I do not remember.

Q. It was during that time he made that remark?

A. Yes.

Q. Was he an active promoter of the movement?

A. I think he was.

Q. Has he any connection with the Government to-day?

A. No, except he is one of the Commissioners in Washington.

Q. You have been in previous revolutions here?

A. I have been in the Wilcox revolution. I took quite a prominent part in its suppression. I was one of the ministers at the time.

Q. You had a conversation with Mr. Carter about the time the proclamation was being read?

A. Yes.

Q. You were somewhat anxious as to whether or not you would be supported by United States troops?

A. Yes.

Q. Did you express any fear in the presence of Mr. Carter?

A. Well, no man likes to tell he was afraid.

Q. I do not mean in a cowardly sense.

A. Well, with others, I was convinced that we were in a position of danger.

Q. What did Mr. Carter say?

A. He gave me to understand that we would be protected.

Q. By United States troops?

A. Yes; and when we were not protected by them I wanted to know the reason why.

Q. Do you mean by that that you expected them to march over?

A. I was under the impression that they would.

Q. What did you accomplish by that first visit to the station-house — any agreement?

A. We accomplished this — that it was a virtual giving up.

Q. What was said? What did the ministers say?

A. This is my impression of it to-day: That if they had

only to contend with the Provisional Government, and the forces of the Provisional Government, that they would not give up. That was the impression that I gathered from them — that they felt themselves equal to the occasion so far as the Provisional Government went.

Q. Then having that sort of feeling, what did they propose to do?

A. They proposed to immediately deliver up. Then they went up, four of them, and had a parley with Mr. Dole and the Provisional Government. They agreed to desist, but said they must go to the Queen and get her to confer with them.

Q. So far as they were concerned they were willing to yield, provided the Queen was?

A. Yes. Then I went along with them to the Palace. We all met in the Blue Room. There were present the Queen, two young princes, the four ministers, Judge Widdeman, Paul Neumann, J. O. Carter, E. C. McFarland, and myself. We went over between 4 and 5 and remained until 6 discussing the situation.

Q. In that conversation you asked for a surrender of the forces, and the ministers advised it?

A. The different ones spoke and they all recommended it. Each one spoke. At first Judge Widdeman was opposed to it, but he finally changed his mind on the advice of Mr. Neumann. Mr. Neumann advised yielding. Each one advised it.

Q. Was this advice of Neumann and the Cabinet based on the idea that the Queen would have to contend with the United States forces as well as the forces of the Provisional Government?

A. It was the Queen's idea that she could surrender pending a settlement at Washington, and it was on that condition that she gave up. If I remember right, I spoke to her also. I said she could surrender or abdicate under protest.

Q. And that the protest would be considered at a later period at Washington?

A. At a later period.

Q. Did the Cabinet in recommending her to yield to the Provisional Government give her to understand that they supposed that the American minister and the United States troops were in sympathy with the Provisional Government or with the Committee of Public Safety?

A. I know it was the Queen's idea that Mr. Stevens was in sympathy with this movement.

THE HAWAIIAN INCIDENT 47

Q. But I am asking now as to what reasons the ministers gave for her acquiescence.
A. It was their idea that it was useless to carry on — that it would be provocative of bloodshed and trouble if she persisted in this matter longer; that it was wiser for her to abdicate under protest and have a hearing at a later time; that the forces against her were too strong.
Q. Did they indicate the United States forces at all in any way?
A. I do not remember their doing so.
Q. Do you know whether or not at that time they were under the impression that the United States forces were in sympathy with the revolution?
A. Beyond an impression I know nothing definite.
Q. What was the result of this conference with the Queen? What was agreed on?
A. She signed a document surrendering her rights to the Provisional Government under protest.
Q. Is this the protest on page 22, Ex. Doc. No. 76, 52d Cong., 2d Sess.?
A. Yes. This was written out by Mr. Neumann and J. O. Carter while we were present. She was reluctant to agree to this, but was advised that the whole subject would come up for final consideration at Washington.
Q. Did you at the time consent to recommend this proposition or not?
A. I was there as a member of the Provisional Government, but I did not advise as to the wording of it. I did tell her that she would have a perfect right to be heard at a later period.
Q. By the United States Government?
A. Yes.
Q. You yourself, at that time, before consulting with your colleagues, were favorably impressed with that settlement?
A. Well, it was the only settlement that could be brought about. Personally I was satisfied with it.
Q. And you took that back to the Provisional Government?
A. Yes.
Q. And they rejected it?
A. It was received and indorsed by Mr. Dole.
Q. Now, was there any message sent to the Queen after that?
A. No.
Q. No message declaring that they would not accept it?
A. No.

Q. The surrender was then made on that proposition?
A. Yes; well, then she sent down word through Mr. Peterson to Mr. Wilson to deliver up the station-house. That wound up the whole affair. We immediately took possession of it. It was not delivered up until after this conference.

Q. Now, how long after that was it before the Provisional Government was recognized?
A. Mr. Stevens sent Cadet Pringle, his aid, and Captain Wiltse sent one of his officers, to personally examine the building and report if the Provisional Government was in actual possession of the Government building. That was done that afternoon.

Q. What time?
A. Between 4 and 5.

Q. What time was the interview with the Queen?
A. After 4, and ended at 6.

Q. You took reply?
A. Mr. Neumann took the reply to Mr. Dole.

Q. Now, when this interview was going on between you, the Cabinet ministers, and the Queen, it was known then that the Government had been recognized?
A. That the Queen knew it? I do not think she was told. I no not remember of it being spoken of.

Q. Didn't you know it?
A. I think I knew it.

Q. Didn't these ministers know it then?
A. They may have been present. I cannot say. The Provisional Government were all present when Mr. Stevens recognized it as the *de facto* Government.

Q. What I mean is this: Before you took the message of the Queen back — this protest — the Provisional Government had been recognized?
A. Yes; that is my impression.

Q. Had that been done at the time you left the Government house to go with the Cabinet ministers to talk with the Queen?
A. If my memory serves me right, it had.

Q. Did not the Cabinet officers know of it at this time?
A. I cannot say.

Q. What do you know about the contents of the constitution she wanted to proclaim?
A. It is too long to write down. I can tell you my connection with it.

Q. Have you seen it?
A. No.

Q. What is the aspiration of the native mind as to the form of government, etc., etc. ?

. . . .

TUESDAY, May 2, 1893.

Q. Mr. Damon, at the time of the writing of the protest of the Queen on the 17th day of January, 1893, signed by herself and ministers, had the Provisional Government been recognized by the American minister, Mr. Stevens ?
A. It is my impression that it had been, but I cannot say positively.
Q. Would the conversation you had with the Queen on that day aid you in determining that fact ?
A. I do not think it would.
Q. In referring to Mrs. Wilson living with the Queen, in a previous part of this statement, did you mean to say that she stayed with her at night ?
A. I mean to say that she was with the Queen a great deal of the time — both day and night.
Q. As a companion ?
A. Yes; as a personal friend and companion.
Q. But where do you suppose she slept — at the bungalow or Palace ?
A. My impression is that her quarters were with her husband in the bungalow.

I have carefully read through the foregoing and pronounce it an accurate report of the two interviews between Mr. Blount and myself.

S. M. DAMON.

To supplement Mr. Damon's testimony, the Queen's protest is here given: [31]

I, Liliuokalani, by the grace of God and under the Constitution of the Hawaiian Kingdom, Queen, do hereby solemnly protest against any and all acts done against myself and the Constitutional Government of the Hawaiian Kingdom by certain persons claiming to have established a Provisional Government of and for this Kingdom.

That I yield to the superior force of the United States of America, whose minister plenipotentiary, His Excellency John L. Stevens, has caused United States troops to be landed at Honolulu, and declared that he would support the said Provisional Government.

Now, to avoid any collision of armed forces, and perhaps the loss of life, I do, under this protest, and impelled by said force, yield my authority until such time as the Government of the United States shall, upon the facts being presented to it, undo the action of its representative, and reinstate me in the authority which I claim as the constitutional Sovereign of the Hawaiian Islands.

Done at Honolulu, this 17th day of January, A.D. 1893.

LILIUOKALANI, R.
SAMUEL PARKER,
Minister of Foreign Affairs.
WM. H. CORNWELL,
Minister of Finance.
JNO. F. COLBURN,
Minister of the Interior.
A. P. PETERSON,
Attorney-General.

S. B. DOLE, Esq., and others,
Composing the Provisional Government of the Hawaiian Islands.

(Indorsed) Received by the hands of the late Cabinet this 17th day of January, A.D. 1893. (Signed) Sanford B. Dole, chairman of the Executive Council of Provisional Government.

Let us now go back for a while and examine the all-important question in regard to Mr. Stevens's recognition of the Government. Perhaps nothing is more remarkable in this whole transaction than the account given by Mr. Stevens himself of his actions at the time of recognizing the Provisional Government, under what was practically a cross-examination by Senator Gray. By this recognition the destinies of 90,000 inhabitants of the Sandwich Islands were to be affected; these were to be brought under a totally different form of government, with possible annexation to the United States, and with all that implied. Upon this latter country was to be thrown the burden of many troublesome and perplexing questions which must arise from annexation and which cannot be ignored, and there would be added to its population some 25,000 to 30,000 native Hawaiians, and some 30,000 Chinese and Japanese; in short, an endless series of important and far-reaching consequences rested upon the word which Mr. Stevens was about to speak.

Mr. Stevens, as he says himself, was no novice in these matters, and he must have known and did know that his duty as a United States minister to a foreign and friendly country demanded of him calm and deliberate judgment, and the exercise of perfect good faith.

Now, when Mr. Stevens was forming a judgment as to the existence of a *de facto* Government, what need was there of excessive haste? If the Provisional Government really existed and was in possession, the mere recognition as such could not add to its validity. It was as much a *de facto* Government without recognition as it was with recognition. To test this, it may be asked whether that Government was any less established before it was recognized, for instance, by the Portuguese consul the next day, or was it any more established after such recognition?

The recognition of the Provisional Government when the revolution was only partly accomplished would, of course, be of the greatest moral force to assist in bringing it to a finish by the surrender of the Queen; but if, at any time during the day, the revolution was successfully accomplished, then this Provisional Government was in fact a Government; it stood upon its own rights before the world, and it could have gone on exercising them if Mr. Stevens had remained in Hilo, and had said neither yea nor nay. If it was not really and truly a *de facto* Government it ought not to have been recognized at all.

If Mr. Stevens was feeling unwell or was weary, why could he not have waited till next day, and then calmly and coolly, and with due deliberation, have examined the position of affairs for himself? The request for recognition expressly says that the Provisional Government was in control of the city. The United States troops were stationed part at the Consulate and part near the Government building; they were all ready and prepared " to protect life and property " whenever either was assailed, and according to Mr. Stevens that was the very purpose for which they were brought on shore. What, then, was the need of hasty or precipitate action?

If we suppose Mr. Stevens to have been acting in this matter in entire good faith, wishing simply to do equal and exact justice to all, this question would be difficult to answer. But if this recognition was to be used as a means to force a reluctant Queen to surrender her troops and her throne without a struggle, then the recognition was of the greatest importance to the revolutionists, and we can perfectly understand why they were in such desperate haste to receive it. Whether this was the object for which recognition was so hastily asked and granted, and whether the purpose of such recognition was fulfilled, the reader will judge from the evidence before him. The testimony of Mr. Stevens most particularly bearing upon the recognition is now given.[32]

Senator GRAY. — When you sent the note of recognition to the Provisional Government, to whom did you send it?

Mr. STEVENS. — I have no doubt I sent it to the Minister of Foreign Affairs. Mr. Dole, under their organization, was President and Minister of Foreign Affairs. Of course, the official usage is to send such notes to the Minister of Foreign Affairs. I have no doubt I sent it to the Minister of Foreign Affairs. I presume I conformed to the custom.

The CHAIRMAN. — Had you previously heard of the proclamation of the Provisional Government?

Mr. STEVENS. — Yes.

Senator GRAY. — Had you a copy of that proclamation?

Mr. STEVENS. — I cannot say.[1]

---

[1] The letter to Mr. Stevens asking recognition expressly refers to the proclamation, "a copy of which is hereby enclosed for your consideration."

The important part of this proclamation was as follows:

" 1. The Hawaiian monarchical system of government is hereby abrogated.

" 2. A Provisional Government for the control and management of public affairs and the protection of the public peace is hereby established, to exist until terms of union with the United States of America have been negotiated and agreed upon."

Senator GRAY. — Had you read that proclamation?
Mr. STEVENS. — I cannot say that I had.
Senator GRAY. — Could you say that you had not?
Mr. STEVENS. — I could not say that I had not.
Senator GRAY. — Was any proclamation sent to you?
Mr. STEVENS. — Things had to be done very rapidly that afternoon. I had no clerk and I was a sick man, and it was impossible for me to make notes. I have no doubt I received the proclamation.
Senator GRAY. — And you cannot say one way or the other whether a copy of that proclamation was sent to you?
Mr. STEVENS. — I cannot; I presume so. Mr. Pringle brought me information, and so did Mr. Carter, and so did others. I had it in various ways.
Senator GRAY. — Were you aware when it was sent to you that the terms of the Provisional Government were not settled until there was annexation to the United States?
Mr. STEVENS. — I did not understand that.
Senator GRAY. — Were you aware that the proclamation was so made?
Mr. STEVENS. — I never heard of it.
Senator GRAY. — Never heard of the proclamation?
Mr. STEVENS. — I did not know that that was the limit of the Provisional Government until this controversy of Mr. Thurston and Mr. Gresham.
Senator GRAY. — When you were acting for the Government, you did not understand the terms in which the Government you were about to recognize had been proclaimed?
Mr. STEVENS. — The only fact that I took under consideration was that it was a *de facto* Government, and if that *de facto* Government had proposed to annex to Mormondom, I should have recognized it. I should have recognized it regardless of any ulterior purposes of that Government.
Senator GRAY. — In this important condition of affairs in Hawaii, you did not consider it necessary to examine the terms on which that Government was established?
Mr. STEVENS. — All I wanted to know was that it was a *de facto* Government, and that information I had.
Senator GRAY. — Where did you get it, except from the proclamation?
Mr. STEVENS — From parties who came from the Government house and informed me, and I presume they sent a copy of the proclamation.
Senator GRAY. — Who were they?
Mr. STEVENS. — My impression is that Charles Carter was

one and Mr. Pringle was another. Mr. Pringle was acting as my aid. Others gave me the information. Which one brought it first I could not swear. I think I first received the information from my daughter.

Senator GRAY. — What time in the afternoon did this fact come to your knowledge, that the Provisional Government had been proclaimed?

Mr. STEVENS. — Probably — I cannot say positively; I did not look at the watch — half-past 2 or 3. It might have been earlier or a little later.

Senator GRAY. — By whom did you send your note of recognition?

Mr. STEVENS. — That I cannot say positively.

Senator GRAY. — Did you send it back by the messenger from the Provisional Government?

Mr. STEVENS. — I sent it by some one whom I considered a reliable messenger.

Senator GRAY. — And you cannot say who it was?

Mr. STEVENS. — No; I cannot say that. It may have been Mr. Pringle, or it may have been one of the clerks in the foreign office

Senator GRAY. — How soon after you were notified of the fact that the Provisional Government had been proclaimed that you sent your note of recognition?

Mr. STEVENS. — That I could not swear positively. I put it on record. I think it was about 5 o'clock. Mrs. Stevens and my daughter think that when this gentleman, meaning Hopkins, called with the note from the Queen's recent ministers it was later. But not regarding that a vital point I put it down in the records about 5. And the fact that the Chief Justice called on me shortly and said that they had the rumor all through the streets that the American minister had refused to recognize the Provisional Government. He came to see if it were so, and it was about dusk when Judge Judd called, when I said to him I had just recognized. But I put it down as my opinion that it was about 5.

Senator GRAY. — You do not claim to be accurate about that?

Mr. STEVENS. — No; the official records will show that.

Senator GRAY. — Have you the official record?

Mr. STEVENS. — I think that is in Honolulu. I do not know that Mr. Blount has put that on paper. My wife and daughter afterward said they thought it was later.

Senator GRAY. — After the messenger who first came from the Provisional Government to notify you that the Provisional

THE HAWAIIAN INCIDENT 55

Government had been proclaimed, what other intelligence did you receive of its proclamation?

Mr. STEVENS. — Now, I have to answer that in the way I have already answered, that I considered that there was an absolute interregnum between the afternoon of the 14th and the establishment of the Provisional Government, and my relief from the situation was that there was a *de facto* Government. The moment I got information that a *de facto* Government was established and was master of the situation, master of the archives, I thought it was my duty to recognize it, and all the other foreign officials immediately did the same. And the English minister called on the Provisional Government in person before I did.

Senator GRAY. — Recognized it before you did?

Mr. STEVENS. — The English minister in person went before I did and offered his congratulations.

Senator GRAY. — Did you before that get your note?

Mr. STEVENS. — I cannot say. All those members of the official corps knew the circumstances under which the Provisional Government had been constituted as well as I did.

Senator GRAY. — I understood you to say, in answer to that question as to whether you had any information of the proclamation of the Provisional Government than the messenger conveyed to you, although not directly responsive, that it was not necessary, because it was thoroughly understood for the last two or three days there was an interregnum, and that any Government or any proclamation of any set of people would constitute a *de facto* Government.

Mr. STEVENS. — I did not say that. Let me answer it.

Senator GRAY. — What did you say when I asked you in regard to the fact, that it was notorious that there was an interregnum and it was not necessary to have the information?

Mr. STEVENS. — I do not put it in that form. I say that the collapse of all government on the islands took place on the attempted *coup d'état* of the Queen on the 14th, and from that time up to the time the Provisional Government took possession of the Government buildings the only Government was the 1,000 citizens who called the mass meeting, and the presence of ship "Boston" in the harbor. I had got information that I deemed reliable that a Government springing out of that condition of things had become a *de facto* Government, and by the invariable usage of the world I was bound to recognize it.

Senator GRAY. — Then, I suppose, you give that answer as accounting for the fact that you did not need any other information than the first reliable information which you received, that the Provisional Government had been proclaimed?

Mr. STEVENS. — I had the most thorough information on that.

Senator GRAY. — I ask you what that was?

Mr. STEVENS. — I said before, probably by a note. But by various means I got that information perhaps twenty times within an hour.

Senator GRAY. — From whom?

Mr. STEVENS. — The parties who called.

Senator GRAY. — Who were the parties?

Mr. STEVENS. — I will give you one instance. Chief Justice Judd is one of the representative men of the islands. He came, I may say, at 5 or a little later, and he said the rumor had got on the street that I had not recognized the Provisional Government. I am sure during those hours there were many persons who called and talked of what had been done.

Senator GRAY. — Who were the many persons?

Mr. STEVENS. — I could not be positive.

Senator GRAY. — Who was one?

Mr. STEVENS. — I presume that Mr. Dole sent his clerk of the foreign office, and in addition to that Mr. Cooper, Carter, and Pringle, and I presume there were many other persons who told me.

Senator GRAY. — Were they sympathizers with the Provisional Government who told you?

Mr. STEVENS. — They were men who would give me absolute information.

Senator GRAY. — I ask if that was a fact?

Mr. STEVENS. — That was a fact.

Senator GRAY. — You were not out of your house?

Mr. STEVENS. — Not out of my house.

Senator GRAY. — And on this information that the Provisional Government had been proclaimed you sent the note?

Mr. STEVENS. — So soon as I had evidence of the fact.

Senator GRAY. — What fact?

Mr. STEVENS. — The fact that out of that interregnum had sprung a *de facto* Government.

Senator GRAY. — The fact of its being a *de facto* Government is a conclusion?

Mr. STEVENS. — Of which I had to be the judge.

Senator GRAY. — Did you judge that that was the *de facto* Government upon the information that came to you that a Provisional Government had been proclaimed?

Mr. STEVENS. — Only in part. I judged it from the condition of the town and all the circumstances. I knew that the Provisional Government had been talked of for sixty hours, and I had it from many persons. I was living on the principal street, and they would hear it on the street and tell my daughter about it, and would come by in a carriage and tell me.

Senator GRAY. — Had you any knowledge of any other fact in regard to the transactions of that afternoon that bore upon the question at all, except the fact that the Provisional Government had been proclaimed?

Mr. STEVENS. — I knew the fact an hour and a half before. You will see how importantly this fact bears on the situation, the efforts of the Provisional Government to transfer the arms from the store, and the abortive attempt of one of Mr. Wilson's policemen to interfere, and that was all the resistance for sixty hours —

Senator GRAY. — Who told you that?

Mr. STEVENS. — I learned it probably from twenty different sources. I heard the shot.

Senator GRAY. — Tell me the name of some one who told you.

Mr. STEVENS. — I guess my own daughter told me first.

Senator GRAY. — Who told you afterward?

Mr. STEVENS. — That I could not tell, because events passing so rapidly like that, and a hundred men calling on me, it would be impossible to remember who the individual was. But there were many.

Senator GRAY. — Why did you not wait until the next day before you sent the note of recognition?

Mr. STEVENS. — For the reason that a half-century of the study of government on both continents and thirteen years of diplomatic experience would have told me it was right.

Senator GRAY. — That was the result of your study?

Mr. STEVENS. — My study and experience would have told me so.

Senator GRAY. — And your study and experience told you that it was right to recognize that Government within an hour or an hour and a half?

Mr. STEVENS. — I do not accept it in that form.

Senator GRAY. — I ask you as a matter of fact whether you did recognize it within an hour or an hour and a half?

Mr. STEVENS. — I do not think that material; probably within an hour and a half or two hours.

Senator GRAY. — Whether it is material or not, answer the question.

Mr. STEVENS. — I do not know the precise time by the clock.

Senator GRAY. — That is sufficient; you do not know the time; you cannot say whether it was an hour or an hour and a half?

Mr. STEVENS. — It was probably inside of two hours.

Senator GRAY. — Were you well acquainted with Mr. Thurston?

Mr. STEVENS. — Pretty well acquainted with him, because he was a minister of the Government when I went to Honolulu.

Senator GRAY. — Are you well acquainted with W. O. Smith?

Mr. STEVENS. — Passably well. He lived near me, within half a mile. I never had much acquaintance with him; met him occasionally, and as Americans we went to the same church. In the course of a year he and his wife called at our house two or three times.

Senator GRAY. — Did any of these gentlemen, Mr. Thurston, Mr. Smith, — any of them connected with the Committee of Public Safety, — call upon you on Sunday?

Mr. STEVENS. — I have already stated that Mr. Thurston called a few minutes at my house Sunday. I would not know when a gentleman called on me whether he was on the Committee of Safety or not, because I would not know until I saw the list. On Sunday they had not been appointed.

Senator GRAY. — I say, not whom you knew were on the Committee of Safety, but whether any of these gentlemen whom you knew afterward were on the Committee of Safety?

Mr. STEVENS. — I have said that I think that Mr. Thurston called; stopped in five minutes, as he passed down, and I think Judge Hartwell called also. Others called, of both parties, during Sunday?

Senator GRAY. — Did Mr. Damon call?

Mr. STEVENS. — I do not recollect Mr. Damon calling.

. . . .

Senator GRAY. — Did Mr. Damon and Mr. Thurston call on Monday?

Mr. STEVENS. — I have no reliable recollection in that regard. My acquaintance with Mr. Thurston grew out of the fact that he was Minister of the Interior for the first thirteen months of my residence in Honolulu. I knew him officially and privately, for he lived in the part of the city in which the Legation is situated.

Here we find that this gentleman, a United States minister, a trained diplomatist, is unable to give a connected and intelligible account of what took place on the occasion in question. He does not know to whom he sent the note of recognition. Reasoning upon the matter, he has no doubt that he sent it to the Minister of Foreign Affairs, forgetful, apparently, of the fact that the note requesting his signature was signed by Mr. Dole and fourteen others, " members of the Executive and Advisory Councils of the Provisional Government," and did not contain the slightest hint that Mr. Dole was Minister of Foreign Affairs, or that there had been any minister appointed for foreign affairs, or for anything whatever.

He cannot say whether he had a copy of the proclamation. He cannot say whether the proclamation was sent to him, though he presumes it was. He cannot say whether he had or had not read it. He did not know what was the limit of the Provisional Government (in reference to annexation). He is unable to tell who gave him the information that a *de facto* Government had been established, although he has an " impression " upon the subject. He cannot tell how the fact that the Provisional Government had been proclaimed came to his knowledge. He cannot say by whom he sent his note of recognition. He cannot tell positively how long it was after he was notified by the Provisional Government that he sent his note. He says that the English minister called [1] on the Provisional Government before he did, but does not know whether or not that occurred before he got the note requesting recognition.

Though he says that he had the most thorough information that the Provisional Government had been proclaimed,

---

[1] He does not say recognized; that would have been going too far. In point of fact, all the notes of the foreign officials are dated the 18th, the day after, except the English minister's, which was dated the 19th.

he does not tell how he got the information, but "probably" by note; he is not certain. He also got it from many other persons.

Being asked who these persons were, he names one, Chief Justice Judd. But Judge Judd, who was in sympathy with the revolutionists, simply tells him that the rumor had got on the street that he (Stevens) had *not* recognized the Provisional Government. Being asked again who were the persons informing him, he cannot be positive; being asked to name one, he "presumes" that Mr. Dole sent "his clerk of the foreign office;" in addition to that, he names Cooper, Carter, and Pringle, his clerk.

Mr. Cooper was chairman of the meeting that chose the Committee of Safety, and was himself on the committee. Charles Carter was one of the commissioners afterwards sent to the United States to negotiate the treaty, and it will be remembered that he was mentioned by Mr. Damon as saying to him, "After you are in possession of the Government building, the troops will support you." Being asked whether the persons who told him were sympathizers with the Provisional Government, he does not answer plainly yes or no, but contents himself with making an evasive reply. Finally he says that he did not leave the house, so that he did not and could not see for himself what had happened.

The situation, then, on Tuesday, January 17, was this: The Queen herself was at the Palace with a small body of troops; at a short distance south of the Palace was the Government building entirely undefended; directly opposite the Government building, and almost adjoining it, lay the United States troops, fully equipped with Gatling gun, arms, and ammunition. At the station-house were the troops of the Queen.[1]

---

[1] The Queen appears to have had some troops at the "barracks," a short distance from the station-house.

The Committee of Safety, having held their mass meeting, were preparing to make the move which was to result in the dethronement of the Queen, and in making them the *de facto* Government.

Now, it will be remembered that when Mr. Stevens in his letter to Mr. Blaine of March 8, 1892, already cited, wrote up the history of a revolution, as it were, in advance, and asked instructions in case it should take place, he said that there were strong reasons to presume that it would begin with the seizure of the police-station with its arms and ammunitions, which being effected, the royal Palace and the Government building, containing the Cabinet offices and archives, would very soon be captured; a very sensible and judicious suggestion, as it would seem, in case parties were really arrayed against each other, and it was intended to fight the matter out. Until the station-house was captured, the taking of the Palace and Government building would be but a barren victory.

But now times were changed. The actors in this drama did not wish nor intend to fight, and it is curious to observe how Mr. Stevens's views have now changed, and the taking of the station-house becomes entirely unnecessary for the success of a *de facto* Government. Consequently the statement made by Mr. Stevens to Mr. Thurston, according to Mr. W. O. Smith, as we have seen, was this: That whatever Government was established and was actually in possession of the Government building, the executive department and archives, and in possession of the city, that Government would have to be recognized.

Here, then, was a fair understanding all round, and knowing exactly what they must do to receive recognition, the committee were content to let the station-house alone till after recognition; and in accordance with the programme laid down, and Mr. Wilcox having been sent to see if "there was any armed force at the Government building," and it appearing that the coast is clear, they take up their line of march for the Government building, going part one way and part another; this being done as a matter of safety and so as not to attract so much attention. When there, they found, according to Mr. Damon, "scarcely any one except porters;" but there was also a head clerk of a department and a man with a rifle. Some of the clerks and officials also came out of the offices, and this being the audience, the chairman of the committee, Mr. Cooper, began to read the proclamation. It was a somewhat long document, and before it was finished some troops came in from the armory and kept coming until they became, as Mr. Damon puts it, quite a body.[1] A message having come from the station-house, Mr. Damon and Mr. Bolte go down there to have a talk with the Marshal. In the meantime all parties "were extremely nervous as to their personal safety," and of course application was at once made to the commander of the United States troops, who were close by for the purpose, as Mr. Damon supposes, of protecting them. Captain Wiltse appears to have thought that under the circumstances there was no occasion to be "nervous," and sends word that he will remain "passive," very much to Mr. Damon's surprise, who was "nonplussed" by such conduct. He could not imagine why they were not supported by the American troops previous to their own troops coming from the armory.

The Government building, with its offices, archives, and its treasury, being now captured and the proclamation read, the revolutionists had done their part, and it remained for Mr. Stevens to do his. Accordingly notice of what had been done was at once sent him, and an

---

[1] J. H. Soper, an American citizen in command of the forces of the revolutionists, thinks that an hour after the reading of the proclamation there were about one hundred and fifty men.

It is claimed by some of the witnesses that this number was afterwards largely increased.

immediate reply was received. The correspondence is now given: [33]

HONOLULU, HAWAIIAN ISLANDS, Jan. 17, 1893.

SIR: The undersigned, members of the Executive and Advisory Councils of the Provisional Government this day established in Hawaii, hereby state to you that for the reasons set forth in the proclamation this day issued, a copy of which is herewith enclosed for your consideration, the Hawaiian monarchy has been abrogated and a Provisional Government established in accordance with the said above-mentioned proclamation.

Such Provisional Government has been proclaimed, is now in possession of the Government departmental buildings, the archives and the treasury, and is in control of the city. We hereby request that you will, on behalf of the United States of America, recognize it as the existing *de facto* Government of the Hawaiian Islands, and afford to it the moral support of your Government, and, if necessary, the support of American troops to assist in preserving the public peace.

We have the honor to remain your obedient servants,

SANFORD B. DOLE.
J. A. KING.
P. C. JONES.
WILLIAM O. SMITH.
S. M. DAWSON.
JOHN EMMELUTH.
F. W. MCCHESNEY.
W. C. WILDER.
J. A. MCCANDLESS.
ANDREW BROWN.
JAS. F. MORGAN.
HENRY WATERHOUSE.
E. D. TENNEY.
F. J. WILHELM.
W. G. ASHLEY.
C. BOLTE.

His Excellency JOHN L. STEVENS,
United States Minister Resident.

To which Mr. Stevens made this reply: [34]

UNITED STATES LEGATION,
HONOLULU, HAWAIIAN ISLANDS, Jan. 17, 1893.

A Provisional Government having been duly constituted in place of the recent Government of Queen Lilioukalani, and said Provisional Government being in full possession of the Government buildings, the archives and the treasury, and in control of the capital of the Hawaiian Islands, I hereby recognize said Provisional Government as the *de facto* Government of the Hawaiian Islands.

JOHN L. STEVENS,
Envoy Extraordinary and Minister Plenipotentiary of the United States.

Mr. Dole then writes to Mr. Stevens as follows : [35]

GOVERNMENT BUILDING,
HONOLULU, Jan. 17, 1893.

His Excellency JOHN L. STEVENS, *United States Minister Resident:*

SIR : I acknowledge the receipt of your valued communication of this day, recognizing the Hawaiian Provisional Government, and express deep appreciation of the same.

We have conferred with the ministers of the late Government, and have made demand upon the Marshal to surrender the station-house. We are not actually yet in possession of the station-house, but as night is approaching and our forces may be insufficient to maintain order, we request the immediate support of the United States forces, and would request that the commander of the United States forces take command of our military forces so that they may act together for the protection of the city.

Respectfully, etc.,
SANFORD B. DOLE,
Chairman Executive Council.

(Note of Mr. Stevens at the end of the above communication : "The above request not complied with. — STEVENS.")

While matters were in progress, and in the excitement of this sudden movement for the overthrow of the Queen, Mr. Stevens's formula of possession of Government building, archives, etc., seemed to be fully sufficient, and it does not appear to have occurred to the parties that such possession might not fully warrant the recognition; but afterwards, when the matter came to be examined in cooler moments, the absurdity of the recognition, while the station-house was still in the hands of the Queen's troops, began to be perceived. Consequently the attempt was made to have it appear that the recognition took place after the surrender. Thus in their letter to Secretary Foster, dated at Washington, Feb. 11, 1893, the Commissioners, replying to the Queen's protest, say: [36]

Sixth. At the time the Provisional Government took possession of the Government buildings, no American troops or officers were present or took part in such proceedings in any manner whatever. No public recognition was accorded the Provisional Government by the American minister until they were in possession of the Government buildings, the archives and the treasury, supported by several hundred armed men, and after the abdication by the Queen and the surrender to the Provisional Government of her forces.

Secretary Foster, in his report of February 15 to President Harrison, in the course of his narrative of the events in question, and apparently following these statements, writes as follows: [37]

At the time the Provisional Government took possession of the Government buildings, no troops or officers of the United States were present or took any part whatever in the proceedings. No public recognition was accorded to the Provisional Government by the United States minister until after the Queen's abdication and when they were in effective possession of the Government buildings, the archives, the treasury, the barracks, the police-station, and all the potential machinery of the Government.

And he adds:

The Provisional Government of the Hawaiian Islands is, by all usual and proper tests, in the sole and supreme possession of power, and in control of all the resources of the Hawaiian nation, not only through the Queen's formal submission, but through its possession of all the armed forces, arms and ammunitions, public offices and administration of law, unopposed by any adherents of the late Government.

These two last extracts are interesting, not only as showing the apparent readiness of the Administration to take the Commissioners' statements on trust without further examination, but they show what Mr. Foster regarded as the usual and proper tests of a *de facto* Government; namely, " the effective possession of the Government buildings, the archives, the treasury, barracks, the police-station, and all the potential machinery of the Government." And again, the "possession of all the armed forces, arms and ammunition, public offices and administration of law, unopposed by any adherents of the late Government."

However desirable it might have been to push the treaty with the utmost haste, if Mr. Foster had thought it worth while to read the correspondence which has just been given, and could have found time so to do, he never would have written and sent to the President, as a basis for action, the first of the sentences above quoted.

Much testimony has been given by various parties as to the precise time when the station-house was surrendered.

In the course of the afternoon the following note was addressed to Mr. Stevens:[38]

DEPARTMENT OF FOREIGN AFFAIRS,
HONOLULU, Jan. 17, 1893.

His Excellency JOHN L. STEVENS, *Envoy Extraordinary and Minister Plenipotentiary*, etc.:

SIR: Her Hawaiian Majesty's Government, having been informed that certain persons to them unknown have issued proclamation declaring a Provisional Government to exist in opposition to her Majesty's Government, and having pretended to depose the Queen, her Cabinet and Marshal, and that certain treasonable persons at present occupy the Government building in Honolulu with an armed force, and pretending that your Excellency, on behalf of the United States of America, has recognized such Provisional Government, her Majesty's Cabinet asks respectfully, Has your Excellency recognized said Provisional Government? and if not, her Majesty's Government, under the above existing circumstances, respectfully requests the assistance of your Government in preserving the peace of the country.

We have the honor to be your Excellency's obedient servants,

SAMUEL PARKER,
Minister Foreign Affairs.
WM. H. CORNWELL,
Minister of Finance.
JOHN F. COLBURN,
Minister of the Interior.
A. P. PETERSON,
Attorney-General.

In regard to which the following memorandum is here cited.[39]

EXTRACT FROM RECORDS OF THE UNITED STATES LEGATION.

Correspondence with Hawaiian Government.

UNITED STATES LEGATION,
HONOLULU, Jan. 17, 1893.

About 4 to 5 P.M. of this date — am not certain of the precise time — the note on file from the four ministers of the deposed Queen, inquiring if I had recognized the Provisional Government, came to my hands while I was lying sick on the couch. Not far from 5 P.M. — I did not think to look at the watch — I addressed a short note to Hon. Samuel Parker, Hon. Wm. H. Cornwell, Hon. John F. Colburn, and Hon. A. P. Peterson — no longer regarding them ministers — informing them that I had recognized the Provisional Government.

JOHN L. STEVENS,
United States Minister.

It will be seen, then, that before writing their letter to Mr. Stevens, the Queen's ministers had heard of the recognition, and that about 4 to 5 o'clock (if Mr. Stevens is correct) he informed them that the recognition had already taken place.

Mr. Bolte, after speaking of a conversation with one McFarlane, says, in answer to the question "Was this conversation at the barracks, or Government house?" [40]

A. At the station-house. The four ministers, Sam Damon, and I took two hacks and went to the Government house. All said about the same thing, that they would have to give up, but they wanted to enter a protest. Then Sam Damon went with the ministers to the Queen. He reported after he came back that the Queen had said in substance the same thing.

Q. What time was it when they came back?
A. Fully 6 o'clock.
Q. About quarter of an hour before sunset?
A. Yes. Very soon after Billy Cornwell came over bringing the protest that you know of. Mr. Dole acknowledged the receipt of the protest on the back of it, stating the hour, and he then said the Queen would send orders to the station-house that her people should vacate the premises. Very soon after that, Captain Zeigler, with a number of our men, went to the station-house and took possession, and the others went away, leaving their arms.

Q. Who was in command of the station-house?
A. Charles B. Wilson, Marshal.

A statement by Lieutenant Draper, of the "Boston," is now given: [41]

May 5, 1893. Herbert L. Draper, Lieutenant Marine Corps attached to "Boston":

I was at the United States Consulate-general at the time the Provisional Government troops went to the station-house, and it was turned over to them by Marshal Wilson. It was about half-past 7 o'clock. The station-house is near the Consulate-general on the same street. As soon as it happened I telephoned to the ship. I wanted my commanding officer to know, as I regarded it as an especially important thing.

I was the commanding officer at the Consulate-general. There was no other United States officer there at the time excepting myself.

The above is a correct statement.

HERBERT L. DRAPER,
First Lieutenant, U.S. Marine Corps.

To which may be appended the following extract from a letter of Lieutenant Swinburne to Mr. Blount: [42]

About half-past 7 P.M. I was informed by telephone by Lieutenant Draper, who was then in charge of a squad of marines at the United States Consulate, that the citizen troops had taken possession of the police-station and that everything was quiet.

The question of the exact time of the recognition has no special importance, except as bearing upon the question whether it was granted before the surrender of the station-house, and this point is made absolutely clear by Mr. Dole himself, because in the same letter in which he acknowledges the recognition (of which he expresses deep appreciation), he also states that he was not in actual possession of the station-house, though a demand had been made for its surrender. This, if anything can be, is conclusive, though if further evidence were wanted it might be found in the fact that neither in Mr. Dole's letter asking recognition, nor in Mr. Stevens's according it, is the station-house mentioned, though the Government buildings, archives, etc., are duly enumerated, nor in the letter written by Mr. Stevens to Secretary Foster and dated the next day, Thursday the 18th, from which the following is an extract: [43]

The Committee of Public Safety forthwith took possession of the Government buildings, archives and treasury, and installed the Provisional Government at the heads of the respective departments. This being an accomplished fact, I promptly recognized the Provisional Government as the *de facto* Government of the Hawaiian Islands.

Let us look again at this last letter of Mr. Dole's and the circumstances under which it was written. The committee had come up to the Government building, and finding it deserted proceeded to capture it. Recognition is at once demanded and at once accorded. But time flies; night is approaching. Mr. Damon is at the Palace trying to overcome the resistance of the Queen. He may not succeed. The Queen's troops at the station-house still stand to their arms.

Suppose they should attack in the night? This might mean bloodshed, and although Mr. Thurston at the mass meeting was ready to shed his blood and if need be even to die for liberty, yet he is sick and far away, and nobody else seems to have the least idea of dying. In case of attack, what if at that the supreme moment Captain Wiltse should fail them! What if there should have been any misunderstanding between him and Mr. Stevens, as to what was expected of the United States troops! It is now that Mr. Dole throws off all disguise, and again turns with a cry for help to his never-failing friend, and asks for the immediate support of the United States troops, and that Captain Wiltse may take command of their forces in conjunction with his own! With this formidable combination all will be safe.

This moving appeal seems to have been a little too much even for Mr. Stevens, who, however, will do what he can, and replies with his usual promptness and with his inevitable reference to "protection of life and property": [44]

UNITED STATES LEGATION,
HONOLULU, Jan. 17, 1893.

Think Captain Wiltse will endeavor to maintain order and protect life and property, but do not think he would take command of the men of Provisional Government.

Will have him come to help the Legation soon as possible, and take his opinion and inform you as soon as possible.

Yours truly,
JOHN L. STEVENS.

Mr. Dole's fears were not realized. The Queen surrendered, sending to the Provisional Government the following paper signed by herself and her ministers, which was received by Mr. Dole, as appears by his indorsement thereon:

I, Liliuokalani, by the grace of God and under the constitution of the Hawaiian Kingdom, Queen, do hereby solemnly protest against any and all acts done against myself and the constitutional Government of the Hawaiian Kingdom by certain persons claiming to have established a Provisional Government of and for this Kingdom.

That I yield to the superior force of the United States of America, whose minister plenipotentiary, His Excellency John L. Stevens, has caused United States troops to be landed at Honolulu and declared that he would support the said Provisional Government.

Now, to avoid any collision of armed forces and perhaps the loss of life, I do, under this protest, and impelled by said force, yield my authority until such time as the Government of the United States shall, upon the facts being presented to it, undo the action of its representatives and reinstate me in the authority which I claim as the constitutional sovereign of the Hawaiian Islands.

Done at Honolulu this 17th day of January, A.D. 1893.

LILIUOKALANI, R.

(Indorsed) Received from the hands of the late Cabinet, this 17th day of January, 1893.   SANFORD B. DOLE.

Thus there was no fear of further trouble that night.

In a letter to Mr. Willis, dated December 23, 1893, Mr. Dole disposes of Mr. Damon as follows: [45]

Mr. Damon, on the occasion mentioned, was allowed to accompany the Cabinet of the former Government, who had been in conference with me and my associates, to meet the ex-Queen. He went informally, without instructions and without authority to represent the Government, or to assure the ex-Queen "that if she surrendered under protest, her case would afterwards be fairly considered by the President of the United States." Our ultimatum had already been given to the members of the ex-Cabinet who had been in conference with us. What Mr. Damon said to the ex-Queen he said on his individual responsibility and did not report it to us.

If Mr. Damon was "allowed" to meet the Queen, who allowed him except the Provisional Government? He was himself a leading member, and he went to the Palace from the men constituting this Government, then grouped together at the Government building, where Mr. Dole was delivering his "ultimatum" and writing his call for help.

Under these circumstances the Queen had every right to suppose that Mr. Damon was clothed with due authority. When Mr. Dole received the above paper, why did he not then state that Mr. Damon had gone without instructions and without authority, if this was the true state of affairs? Why was he *then* silent, when, if ever, he was called upon to speak?

Before leaving this branch of the subject it is desired to call attention to two pieces of testimony given by Lieutenant Swinburne, who was in command of the troops when landed. The first is as follows: [46]

Senator GRAY. — And you were there, as I understand, under your orders to preserve order?
Mr. SWINBURNE. — To preserve order, to protect the property and lives of Americans.
Senator GRAY. — And if a crowd of people, disorderly or otherwise, should have attempted to arrest or maltreat Mr. Damon, Mr. Dole, or Mr. Carter on that day, you would have protected them?
Mr. SWINBURNE. — It would have depended upon what they were doing.
Senator GRAY. — Suppose they were walking up to the Government building, as they were doing that morning, and they were set upon, would you have protected them?
Mr. SWINBURNE. — If they were going to the Government building?
Senator GRAY. — Yes.
Mr. SWINBURNE. — I should think I would have been called upon to protect them.
Senator GRAY. — I think so.
Mr. SWINBURNE. — They were entitled to the liberty of the streets, but if they were organized as a force —
Senator GRAY. — I say if they were going up to the Government buildings, as they were on that day, and were set upon?
Mr. SWINBURNE. — And if I had been informed, as I was, that this party was going in to take the Government building?

Senator GRAY. — Would you have allowed them to be maltreated or set upon?
Mr. SWINBURNE. — That is a difficult question to answer.
Senator GRAY. — I sympathize with you in it.
Mr. SWINBURNE. — That would be difficult to answer.
Senator GRAY. — I think so.

From this it would appear that if Messrs. Damon, Dole, and Carter were walking up through the street as individuals, they would have been protected. That was easy to decide. But if they were going up to take the Government house, then Lieutenant Swinburne finds the question whether he would have allowed them to be set upon a difficult one. Why difficult? Unless the preventing of the Queen's troops from attacking the revolutionists had been contemplated, what could have been easier than the answer that he was on shore to protect life and property, and not to interfere with either party?

If the lieutenant could have said this truthfully, why should he not have said it?

But this was not the only difficult question the chief officer was called upon to answer. The following appears in his testimony: [47]

The next morning about 11 o'clock, while standing outside the camp, the English minister and the Portuguese minister came along.
Senator GRAY. — When was that?
Mr. SWINBURNE. — Wednesday morning. The English minister stopped and notified me that he had just been to notify the Provisional Government that he would recognize them as the *de facto* Government, pending advice from his Government; but he said, as a sort of parenthesis, "I found it necessary to ask them, if they were the *de facto* Government, why it was necessary to bring foreign troops on the soil." He expected an answer from me. I looked as if I had no answer to give, and he looked at me a few minutes and went on.

One is here reminded of Cicero's oft-quoted remark that he wondered how two augurs could look each other in the face without laughing. We can imagine the smile that must have stolen over the countenances of these gentlemen, as they stood looking at each other for a few minutes, after the English minister's very significant question and Lieutenant Swinburne's still more significant silence.

It may not be wholly out of place to say here that the Provisional Government were duly grateful for the "protection to life and property" which the United States troops had given, as appears by the following resolutions:[48]

Be it resolved by the Provisional Government of the Hawaiian Islands as follows:

That the thanks of this Government are due and are hereby tendered to Gilbert C. Wiltse, captain in the United States Navy, now commanding the United States steamship-of-war "Boston," for his gallant, well-timed, and judicious conduct in protecting life and property in the city of Honolulu, upon the occasion of his landing his forces at the request of the United States envoy extraordinary and minister plenipotentiary; that like thanks are due and are hereby tendered to the officers and men of the United States Navy who composed the landing force from the "Boston," and whose discipline, forbearance, and gentlemanly conduct under circumstances of considerable annoyance, and in several instances of much exasperation, entitle them to the gratitude of the people of the Hawaiian Islands.

There can be no doubt that Captain Wiltse is a brave and capable officer; but seeing that neither he nor his officers nor men were called upon to make the slightest exhibition of their courage, and in view of the fact that the Committee of Safety did their best to postpone the landing, the epithets "gallant" and "well-timed," as applied to his conduct by the Provisional Government, must have struck Captain Wiltse as somewhat curious.

It might be fairly supposed that the Provisional Government, which was supposed to be, in the language of Mr. Foster already quoted, "in the sole and supreme possession of power, and in control of all the resources of the Hawaiian nation, and in the possession of all the armed forces, arms and ammunition, public offices, and all the potential machinery of the Government," might have contrived to run along without asking further aid from Mr. Stevens or the United States, if it were only for the looks of the thing. But not so; "protection for life and property" was still needed, the old formula being still advanced; and in less than a fortnight from the dethronement of the Queen an appeal is made to Mr. Stevens not only for protection to life and property, but this time for protection to the Government of the Hawaiian Islands itself. Here is the correspondence:[49]

HONOLULU, HAWAIIAN ISLANDS, Jan. 31, 1893.

SIR: Believing that we are unable to satisfactorily protect life and property, and to prevent civil disorders to Honolulu and throughout the Hawaiian Islands, we hereby, in obedience to the instructions of the Advisory Council, pray that you will raise the flag of the United States of America for the protection of the Hawaiian Islands for the time being, and to that end we hereby confer upon the Government of the United States, through you, freedom of occupation of the public buildings of this Government, and of the soil of this country, so far as may be necessary for the exercise of such protection, but not interfering with the administration of public affairs by this Government.

We have, etc.,
SANFORD B. DOLE,
President of the Provisional Government of the Hawaiian Islands and Minister of Foreign Affairs.
J. A. KING,
Minister of Interior.
P. C. JONES,
Minister of Finance.
WILLIAM O. SMITH,
Attorney-General.

His Excellency JOHN L. STEVENS,
Envoy Extraordinary and Minister Plenipotentiary of the United States.

Mr. Stevens is quite ready and willing, and takes immediate action:[50]

UNITED STATES LEGATION,
HONOLULU, Feb. 1, 1893.

SIR : The Provisional Government of the Hawaiian Islands having duly and officially expressed to the undersigned the fear that said Government may be unable to protect life and property, and to prevent civil disorder in Honolulu, the capital of said Hawaiian Islands, request that the flag of the United States may be raised for the protection of the Hawaiian Islands, and to that end confer on the United States, through the undersigned, freedom of occupation of the public buildings of the Hawaiian Government and the soil of the Hawaiian Islands, so far as may be necessary for the exercise of such protection, but not interfering with the administration of the public affairs by said Provisional Government.

I hereby ask you to comply with the spirit and terms of the request of the Hawaiian Provisional Government, and to that end to use all the force at your command, in the exercise of your best judgment and discretion, you and myself awaiting instructions from the United States Government at Washington.

I am, sir, etc.,
JOHN L. STEVENS,
*Envoy Extraordinary and Minister
Plenipotentiary of the United States.*

Capt. G. C. WILTSE,
Commander of the U.S. Ship " Boston."

Lieutenant Swinburne gives us an interesting account of the ceremonies attending the raising of the flag:[51]

At half-past 8 the battalion was paraded, the captain arrived and handed me the orders, a copy of which is there, and dated the 1st of February. He ordered me to take charge of the Government building, the flag to be hoisted at 9 o'clock. I marched down with the battalion. At the Government building I found all the members of the Advisory Council and the members of the Cabinet of the Provisional Government. The three companies of troops were drawn up on the three sides of the square. We marched in and were drawn up in front of the building, and then by direction of the captain the adjutant read the proclamation of the minister establishing a protectorate over the islands, pending negotiations with the United

States. As I understand, that was at the request of the Provisional Government. Then the American flag was hoisted and saluted. After the American flag was hoisted the Hawaiian flag was hoisted.

Senator GRAY. — How was the American flag saluted?

Mr. SWINBURNE. — The troops presented arms, and three flourishes of the trumpets were given.

Senator GRAY. — Was a salute fired from the ship?

Mr. SWINBURNE. — A salute of 21 guns was fired from the ship.

Senator GRAY. — What was the salute from the ship?

Mr. SWINBURNE. — The national salute.

The CHAIRMAN. — And then you faced about —

Mr. SWINBURNE. — Faced about and gave the same honors to the Hawaiian flag.

The CHAIRMAN. — Was any salute fired?

Mr. SWINBURNE. — No salute was fired. Then the building was turned over to my custody, and the Provisional Government's troops marched out.

In the further course of his testimony Lieutenant Swinburne throws a bit of side-light upon the then existing state of things: [52]

So two days passed, when President Dole came to me and said he would like to have the Government building opened, that the court might be held, and to that end he would like to have the sentry removed from the front gate during the hours from 9 till 4.

The CHAIRMAN. — What court?

Mr. SWINBURNE. — The Supreme Court. I suggested that it would be better to go further than that, to remove all sentries for the time, so as not to have the appearance of keeping anybody away, which was done. All the sentries were taken from the public building from 9 to 4, all the gates were opened, and the court held its sessions.

From which it would appear that the sovereign and independent Provisional Government of Hawaii, then in treaty for annexation with the United States, could not even open its courts, without the consent of an officer of the United States Navy.

Five commissioners of the Provisional Government left for Washington on Friday, January 20, with full power to treat for the annexation of the Sandwich Islands to the United States. Mr. Stevens gives them a good send-off: [53]

MR. STEVENS TO MR. FOSTER.

UNITED STATES LEGATION,
HONOLULU, Jan. 19, 1893. [Received February 3.]

SIR: The Provisional Government of Hawaii, by special steamer, send a commission to Washington with full powers to negotiate with the Government of the United States. It is composed of six[1] representative men of the highest respectability: Hon. William C. Wilder is the president and chief manager of the Inter-island Steamship Company, running steamers among the islands, and he has large property interests in Honolulu. Hon. C. M. [surname omitted] is a leading lumber merchant, doing business with Puget Sound and Oregon, born here of the best American stock. Hon. L. A. Thurston is one of the most if not *the* most talented and influential man on the islands, and is of the highest respectability. He and his father were born on the islands, of Connecticut parentage. Though a young man, he was the leading member of the reform Cabinet from July, 1887, to 1890.

Hon. William H. Castle is a lawyer of eminence, born on the islands, of western New York parentage, his father still living here at the age of eighty-four, having resided in Honolulu nearly half a century, and for many years exercised a large influence here. Mr. Charles P. Carter is the son of the recent Hawaiian minister at Washington, Hon. H. P. Carter, and is an accomplished and most reliable gentleman, American to the core, and has a Michigan wife. Hon. Mr. Marsden is of English birth, is a prominent business man, and a noble in the Legislature.

These six commissioners represent a large preponderating proportion of the property-holders and commercial interests of these islands. They are backed by the influences which will enable them to fully carry out their agreements with the United States Government.

I am, sir, etc.,

JOHN L. STEVENS.

---

[1] A mistake; it should be five.

It will be remembered that three of these gentlemen, Messrs. Thurston, Wilder, and Castle, were members of the Committee of Safety and of the Provisional Government.

The Commissioners arrived in Washington February 3, and on the same day opened a correspondence with Secretary Foster, informing him of their appointment, and making, among other statements, the following:[54]

> And also the said Commissioners are instructed and fully authorized and empowered by the said Provisional Government to negotiate a treaty between the said Provisional Government of the Hawaiian Islands and the Government of the United States of America, by the terms of which full and complete political union may be secured between the United States of America and the Hawaiian Islands.

On the 4th of February an outline of the proposed treaty was sent to Mr. Foster, and on the 15th Mr. Foster sent the treaty agreed upon to President Harrison, who upon the same day transmitted it to the Senate, stating that he did not deem it necessary to discuss at any length the conditions which had resulted in this decisive action, and with the recommendation already referred to, that it should be promptly acted upon. The treaty, however, remained with the Senate till Mr. Cleveland withdrew it.

In the meantime, when the Commissioners left Honolulu on the "Claudine," the Queen desired to send agents of her own on the same steamer to lay her side of the case before the President. This, however, was refused, and it was not till February 1st that her attorney and envoy, Mr. Paul Neumann, started for Washington.[1] The

---

[1] In their letter to Secretary Foster under date of Feb. 11, 1893, the Commissioners say:[55]

"As the Provisional Government had allowed a mail to be sent by the chartered steamer, they did not consider that there was any reason for financially assisting the Queen in forwarding to Washington an agent hostile to the Government and its objects."

Queen, however, was allowed to use the mail, and she sent the following letter to Mr. Harrison: [57]

His Excellency BENJAMIN HARRISON, *President of the United States:*

MY GREAT AND GOOD FRIEND: It is with deep regret that I address you on this occasion. Some of my subjects, aided by aliens, have renounced their loyalty and revolted against the constitutional Government of my Kingdom. They have attempted to depose me and to establish a Provisional Government in direct conflict with the organic law of this Kingdom. Upon receiving incontestable proofs that His Excellency the minister plenipotentiary of the United States aided and abetted their unlawful movement and caused United States troops to be landed for that purpose, I submitted to force, believing that he would not have acted in that manner unless by authority of the Government which he represents.

This action on my part was prompted by three reasons: the futility of a conflict with the United States, the desire to avoid violence and bloodshed and the destruction of life and property, and the certainty which I feel that you and your Government will right whatever wrongs may have been inflicted upon us in the premises. In due time a statement of the true facts relating to this matter will be laid before you, and I live in the hope that you will judge uprightly and justly between myself and my enemies.

This appeal is not made for myself personally, but for my people, who have hitherto always enjoyed the friendship and protection of the United States.

My opponents have taken the only vessel which could be obtained here for the purpose, and hearing of their intention to send a delegation of their number to present their side of this conflict before you, I requested the favor of sending by the same vessel an envoy to

---

This might appear to be a case where the decision was a very prudent one, but the reason alleged hardly sufficient. Seeing that the Provisional Government had taken the Queen's treasury and all the money in it, it really seems as if a little financial aid would not have been out of place.

"The CHAIRMAN. — Was there any actual capture of the money by the Provisional Government?

"Mr. MCCANDLESS. — The information was that they went up there to inquire for the ministers, the Advisory and Executive Councils. Of course it merged right from the Committee of Safety into them. They asked for the Queen's ministers, and they were not in there, and they asked for the chief clerk, Mr. Hassinger, and demanded the keys, and they were turned over.

"The CHAIRMAN. — That carried with it the custody of the money?

"Mr. MCCANDLESS. — Yes, and of the Government departments — all the affairs of the Government." [56]

you to lay before you my statement as the facts appear to myself and my loyal subjects.

This request has been refused, and I now ask you that in justice to myself and to my people that no steps be taken by the Government of the United States until my cause can be heard by you. I shall be able to despatch an envoy about the 2d day of February, as that will be the first available opportunity hence, and he will reach you with every possible haste, that there may be no delay in the settlement ot this matter.

I pray you, therefore, my good friend, that you will not allow any conclusions to be reached by you until my envoy arrives.

I beg to assure you of the continuance of my highest consideration.

 (Signed)   LILIUOKALANI, R.

This letter is not introduced as evidence of the statements therein contained, but only as a part of the record. Mr. Harrison's acts and motives are not in issue here and will not be discussed; but it is important to know to what his attention had been called at the time he sent his message to the Senate. It does not appear that the slightest notice was ever taken of this letter, or that Mr. Neumann's story was ever heard either by Mr. Harrison or by any one connected with his administration. The above letter having been sent, and Mr. Neumann afterwards being about to leave Honolulu, Mr. Stevens gives him also a good send-off, as will appear from the following extract from his letter to Mr. Foster, dated January 26: [58]

        UNITED STATES LEGATION,
         HONOLULU, Jan. 26, 1893.

SIR: By the steamer taking this despatch goes Mr. Paul Neumann to Washington, the attorney of the desposed Queen. Nominally he may make at the Department of State a "protest" as to the way his client lost her crown. In reality his mission is to get a large fee out of whatever sum it is supposed may be paid by the treaty of annexation to the fallen monarch and the crown princess. This attorney, as the Hawaiian Commissioners now in Washington may inform you, was a former resident of San Francisco, where he had and still has an unsavory reputation. For years his influence in politics here has been pernicious. He was a boon companion of the debased Kalakaua, the recent king, shared in his corruptions, and is reputed to have won at cards the money of the weak monarch.[1]

He arrived in Washington February 11, at which time it may be assumed that the treaty of annexation had been practically agreed upon by the commissioners and Mr. Foster, this being only four days before it was sent in for ratification.

Thus the matter stood until Mr. Cleveland was inaugurated in March, 1893. When Mr. Cleveland took this matter into consideration, some things he must necessarily have known. He knew that Hawaii had been a friendly nation; that a few months before, thirteen individuals naming themselves a Committee of Safety had called together a meeting of the inhabitants of Honolulu, at which certain resolutions were passed; that that same day United States troops had been landed against the protest of the authorities, and that the next day the Queen was deposed and a Provisional Government organized, which was immediately recognized by the United States minister; that two days afterwards Commissioners for annexation were on their way to Washington, and that the Queen had sent the letter cited above; that the resolutions passed by the mass meeting from which the Commissioners professed to derive their power said no word about dethroning the Queen or of annexation, and that so far as official documents went there was nothing to show that any living soul upon the island either had, or could have had, the slightest opportunity to express assent to or disapproval of the action the Commissioners were about to take, or that the Commissioners represented any one except themselves and the other members of the Provisional Government which

---

[1] It is unnecessary to say that Mr. Neumann is very differently spoken of in other portions of the Report.

sent them. He knew also that the statements made by the United States minister and by the Commissioners had been vigorously denied, and that the Queen had made an appeal to his predecessor to take no steps until she had had an opportunity to be heard.

These facts were disputed by no one, and Mr. Cleveland must necessarily have been aware of them. What course, then, should he take? A grave accusation had been made against the United States, involving its honor and reputation, and circumstances which were undisputed gave color to the charge. A great responsibility rested upon the President. Should he let the matter remain as it was, taking the account of the revolution given by the Commissioners, interested as they were, as absolutely true, or should he make inquiry for himself? Mr. Cleveland was a lawyer, and was familiar with that maxim which lies at the foundation of the administration of justice, *Audi alteram partem:* Hear the other side. He determined to hear both sides.[1]

For the purpose of making an investigation he chose Hon. James H. Blount, of Georgia, eighteen years a member of the House of Representatives, where his position as chairman of the Committee of Foreign Affairs had given him great familiarity with international affairs. Mr. Blount was a man of high character and honorable reputation, and upon his leaving Congress all parties, Republicans as well as Democrats, joined in a tribute of praise such as seldom falls to the lot of any public man.[2]

---

[1] The treaty involved, among other things, a question of money; it proposed to give the Queen $20,000 per year, and the Princess Kaiulani, the next heir to the throne, the gross sum of $150,000, conditioned upon their submission in good faith to the United States and to the local Government, so that the private interests of both were to some extent involved. Why these or any other sums should be paid if the Queen was rightfully deposed is not explained.

[2] Mr. Hitt, of Illinois, of the Republican party, made the following remarks:

" But I cannot see the time approach when he [Mr. Blount] is to leave our hall without heartily joining, as one member of the House, with the honorable gentle-

The object of Mr. Blount's mission is given in the following paragraphs from Mr. Gresham's instructions : [60]

DEPARTMENT OF STATE,
WASHINGTON, March 11, 1893.

Hon. JAMES H. BLOUNT, *etc.* :

SIR: The situation created in the Hawaiian Islands by the recent deposition of Queen Liliuokalani and the erection of a Provisional Government demands the fullest consideration of the president, and in order to obtain trustworthy information on this subject, as well as for the discharge of other duties herein specified, he has decided to despatch you to the Hawaiian Islands as his special commissioner, in which capacity you will herewith receive a commission and also a letter, whereby the President accredits you to the president of the Executive and Advisory Councils of the Hawaiian Islands.

The comprehensive, delicate, and confidential character of your mission can now only be briefly outlined, the details of its execution being necessarily left, in a great measure, to your good judgment and wise discretion.

You will investigate and fully report to the President all the facts you can learn respecting the condition of affairs in the Hawaiian Islands, the causes of the revolution by which the Queen's Government was overthrown, the sentiment of the people toward existing authority, and, in general, all that can fully enlighten the President touching the subjects of your mission.

To enable you to fulfil this charge, your authority in all matters touching the relations of this Government to the existing or other Government of the Islands, and the protection of our citizens therein, is paramount, and in you alone, acting in coöperation with the commander of the naval forces, is vested full discretion and power to determine when such forces should be landed or withdrawn.

---

man from Indiana [Mr. Holman] in every word he has said in testimony of the personal worth, of the high character, of the industry, the energy, of the honorable gentleman from Georgia; and I will mark most of all that patriotism above party that inspired him in this House, when last year, leading a great committee charged to consider the affairs and interests, not of a part, but of a whole nation, embroiled in a sharp dispute with a foreign power, he rose with the occasion, and proved himself first and altogether a patriot, an American; so that a foreigner looking down from the gallery upon the hall could neither have told whether he was a Republican or Democrat, but would have known that he was in every fibre an American."

THE HAWAIIAN INCIDENT

Thus far the action of Mr. Cleveland is confined to the sending of a messenger for the purpose of investigation.

Mr. Blount arrived at Honolulu on the 29th of March, 1893, and left about the 1st of August of that year. While there he busied himself in interviewing a great many people, taking a great deal of testimony, and generally endeavoring with due diligence and in good faith to fulfil the object of his mission, from time to time sending reports of his doings and of his conclusions to Mr. Gresham, together with the evidence upon which these conclusions were based. These reports were not satisfactory to the Provisional Government and its adherents, but they are open to public inspection, and are all set forth in the Report upon the Hawaiian Islands. They convinced Mr. Cleveland, as set forth in his message of Dec. 18, 1893, that the lawful Government of Hawaii was overthrown without the drawing of a sword or the firing of a shot, by a process every step of which was directly traceable to and dependent for its success upon the agency of the United States acting through its diplomatic and naval representatives; that but for the presence of the United States forces in the immediate vicinity and in position to afford all needed protection and support, the committee would not have proclaimed the Provisional Government from the steps of the Government building; that by an act of war committed with the participation of a diplomatic representative of the United States, and without authority of Congress, the Government of a feeble, but friendly and confiding people had been overthrown, and that a substantial wrong had been done, which a regard to our national character, as well as the rights of the injured party, required an effort to repair; that the Queen surrendered not to the Provisional Government, but to the United States; not absolutely and permanently, but temporarily and conditionally, until such time as the facts could be considered by the United States; and that the Provisional Government acquiesced in her surrender in that manner and on those terms, not only by tacit consent, but through the positive acts of some members of that Government who urged her peaceable submission, not merely to avoid bloodshed, but because she could place implicit reliance upon the justice of the United States, and that the whole subject would be finally considered at Washington.

It is assumed here that whatever final judgment may be passed upon the character of the revolution, Mr. Cleveland had, at least, reasonable grounds for the conclusions which he formed. What now should be his next step? That would seem to depend somewhat upon the question whether there are or should be such things as justice and equity in the dealings of nations with each other. In his message Mr. Cleveland gives to this question an affirmative answer, influenced possibly by the words of President Washington, who in his farewell address, a document now regarded as almost sacred, and as containing a most authoritative exposition of true American principles, lays down the following precepts:

Observe good faith and justice towards all nations; cultivate peace and harmony with all. Religion and morality enjoin this conduct, and can it be that good policy does not equally enjoin it? It will be worthy of a free, enlightened, and at no distant period a great nation, to give to mankind the magnanimous and too novel example of a people always guided by an exalted justice and benevolence.[1]

Mr. Cleveland determined to right what he believed was a flagrant wrong, so far as he could within the limited powers

---

[1] See also the following remarks of President McKinley:

"Next to the Declaration of Independence itself, Washington's farewell address is the richest heritage that has come down to us from the Father of the Republic. It is not only a perfect analysis of the spirit of the Constitution, but it is a lofty appeal to true American patriotism, accompanied by words of solemn warning and advice, the wisdom of which has been increasingly demonstrated by added experience of each successive generation."

vested in him as President, although in taking this action he undoubtedly ran counter to the views of Mr. Dole as expressed in his letter to Mr. Willis, of December 23, 1893, in which, after denying each and every one of the allegations of fact referred to in a portion of Mr. Willis's letter, he proceeds as follows:[61]

My position is, briefly, this: If the American forces illegally assisted the revolutionists in the establishment of the Provisional Government, that Government is not responsible for their wrong-doing. It was purely a private matter for discipline between the United States Government and its own officers. There is, I submit, no precedent in international law for the theory that such action of the American troops has conferred upon the United States authority over the internal affairs of this Government. Should it be true, as you have suggested, that the American Government made itself responsible to the Queen, who, it is alleged, lost her throne through such action, that is not a matter for me to discuss, except to submit that if such be the case, it is a matter for the American Government and her to settle between them. This Government, a recognized sovereign power, equal in authority with the United States Government and enjoying diplomatic relations with it, cannot be destroyed by it for the sake of discharging its obligations to the ex-Queen.[1]

Mr. Blount having returned from Honolulu, instructions were given to Mr. Albert S. Willis, then United States minister to the islands, to advise the Queen and her supporters of the President's desire to aid in the restoration of the status existing before the lawless landing of the United States forces at Honolulu on the 16th of

---

[1] The principles here laid down may be tested by stating an extreme case. Suppose that Mr. Stevens, Captain Wiltse, and Mr. Dole had entered into a formal conspiracy; that for a sum of money paid by Mr. Dole, Mr. Stevens and Captain Wiltse had agreed that the Queen should be deposed; that thereupon they landed troops, proceeded to bombard and knock to pieces the Palace and Government house, compelled the surrender of the Queen, and established Mr. Dole and his associates in the Government of Hawaii. It is understood that Mr. Dole in such case would say that the United States and the Queen might settle the matter between themselves, and that the United States might discipline its offending officers, but could take no further action in the premises.

Mr. Dole, in stating his principle of international law, omits reference to the somewhat important fact that his Government almost immediately upon its inception had placed itself under a protectorate of the United States.

January last, if such restoration could be effected upon terms providing for clemency as well as justice to all parties concerned. The conditions suggested contemplated a general amnesty to those concerned in setting up the Provisional Government, and a recognition of all its *bona fide* acts and obligations. In short, they required that the past should be buried, and that the restored Government should reassume its authority as if its continuity had not been interrupted.

In pursuance of these instructions Mr. Willis on the 13th of November [62] made known to the Queen the President's regret that through the unauthorized intervention of the United States she had been obliged to surrender her sovereignty, and his hope that with her consent and coöperation the wrongs done to her and her people might be redressed; and she was asked whether if restored to the throne she would grant full amnesty as to life and property to the members of the Provisional Government, and all who had been instrumental in her overthrow. She refused to make this promise, and the fact of such refusal was immediately made known by Mr. Willis to President Cleveland.[63]

On the 3d of December, 1893, the following additional instructions were sent to Mr. Willis.[64]

[*Telegram.*]

DEPARTMENT OF STATE,
WASHINGTON, December 3, 1893.

SIR: Your despatch, which was answered by steamer on the twenty-fifth of November, seems to call for additional instructions.

Should the Queen refuse assent to the written conditions, you will at once inform her that the President will cease interposition in her behalf, and that while he deems it his duty to endeavor to restore to the sovereign the constitutional government of the islands, his further efforts in that direction will depend upon the Queen's unqualified agreement that all obligations created by the Provisional

Government in a proper course of administration shall be assumed, and upon such pledges by her as will prevent the adoption of any measures of proscription or punishment for what has been done in the past by those setting up or supporting the Provisional Government. The President feels that by our original interference and what followed we have incurred responsibilities to the whole Hawaiian community, and it would not be just to put one party at the mercy of the other.

Should the Queen ask whether, if she accedes to conditions, active steps will be taken by the United States to effect her restoration, or to maintain her authority thereafter, you will say that the President cannot use force without the authority of Congress.

Should the Queen accept conditions, and the Provisional Government refuse to surrender, you will be governed by previous instructions. If the Provisional Government asks whether the United States will hold the Queen to fulfilment of stipulated conditions, you will say the President, acting under dictates of honor and duty as he has done in endeavoring to effect restoration, will do all in his constitutional power to cause observance of the conditions he has imposed.

I am, etc.,
W. Q. GRESHAM.

In a message of Dec. 18, 1893, the President laid all the facts relating to the Hawaiian revolution before Congress, to whose " extended powers and wide discretion " the subject was commended.[65]

In the meantime, upon the same date of this message, the Queen having changed her mind, sent a note to Mr. Willis agreeing that if restored she would grant full pardon and amnesty[1] to all parties concerned in the revolution.[66] Mr. Willis, not being aware that the matter was now in the hands of Congress, immediately informed the

---

[1] Senator Hoar was clearly of opinion that as matter of law the promise of the Queen to grant pardon was in strict violation of the Hawaiian constitution, as appears by his speech in the Senate in January, 1894. He goes on to say:

" Mr. President, there is but one point of sympathy between the present Executive of the United States and the deposed Queen of Hawaii, and that is a purpose on the part of each recklessly to disregard the Constitution of their country — the only difference being that the President of the United States disregards our Constitution recklessly and without provocation, while the Queen of Hawaii, in this instance, proposes to disregard it only before the great temptation of a throne."

Provisional Government of this fact, and asked whether it was willing to abide Mr. Cleveland's decision and yield to the Queen her constitutional authority; to which it replied through Mr. Dole in the negative, as follows: [67]

I am instructed to inform you, Mr. Minister, that the Provisional Government of the Hawaiian Islands respectfully and unhesitatingly declines to entertain the proposition of the United States that it should surrender its authority to the ex-Queen.

All this was at once communicated by Mr. Willis to the President, and by him to Congress. Mr. Gresham finally writes Mr. Willis, Jan. 12, 1894, as follows: [68]

Your reports show that on further reflection the Queen gave her unqualified assent in writing to the conditions suggested, but that the Provisional Government refuses to acquiesce in the President's decision.
The matter now being in the hands of Congress, the President will keep that body fully advised of the situation, and will lay before it from time to time the reports received from you, including your No. 3, heretofore withheld, and all instructions sent to you. In the meantime, while keeping the Department fully informed of the course of events, you will, until further notice, consider that your special instructions upon this subject have been fully complied with.

So ended Mr. Cleveland's effort to restore her Government to the Queen.

In order that the full extent of Mr. Cleveland's offending may be shown, an incident must be referred to which exposed him, and still exposes him, to the severest censure.

We have seen under what circumstances and by what authority, and with what imposing ceremonies, the United States flag was hoisted over the Hawaiian public buildings, and the circumstances must now be mentioned under which it was taken down.

First let us see how the action of Mr. Stevens in raising the flag was received by President Harrison. Mr. Stevens gave immediate notice to Secretary Foster, who on the 14th of February replied as follows: [69]

> DEPARTMENT OF STATE,
> WASHINGTON, Feb. 14, 1893.
>
> Your telegram of the 1st instant has been received, with coincident report from commander of the "Boston." Press telegrams from San Francisco give full details of events of 1st instant, with text of your proclamation. The latter, in announcing assumption of protection of the Hawaiian Islands in the name of the United States, would seem to be tantamount to the assumption of a protectorate over those islands on behalf of the United States, with all the rights and obligations which the term implies. It is not thought, however, that the request of the Provisional Government for protection or your action in compliance therewith contemplated more than the coöperation of the moral and material forces of the United States to strengthen the authority of the Provisional Government, by according to it adequate protection for life and property during the negotiations instituted here, and without interfering with the execution of public affairs. Such coöperation was and is within your standing instructions and those of the naval commanders in Hawaiian waters. So far as your course accords to the *de facto* sovereign Government the material coöperation of the United States for the maintenance of good order and protection of life and property from apprehended disorders, it is commended; but so far as it may appear to overstep that limit by setting the authority of the United States above that of the Hawaiian Government in the capacity of protector, or to impair the independent sovereignty of that Government by substituting the flag and power of the United States, it is disavowed.

Instructions will be sent to naval commanders confirming and renewing those heretofore given them, under which they are authorized and directed to coöperate with you in case of need. Your own instructions are likewise renewed, and you are accordingly authorized to arrange with the commanding officer for the continued presence on shore of such marine force as may be practicable and requisite for the security of the lives and property interests of American citizens and the repression of lawlessness threatening them, whenever in your judgment it shall be necessary so to do, or when such coöperation may be sought for good cause by the Government of the Hawaiian Islands; being, however, always careful to distinguish between these functions of voluntary or accorded protection and the assumption of a protectorate over the Government of the Hawaiian Islands, which the United States have recognized as sovereign, and with which they treat on terms of sovereign equality.

JOHN W. FOSTER.

Here it appears that Mr. Foster regarded the action of Mr. Stevens as tantamount to the establishment of a protectorate, with all the rights and obligations which the terms implied.[1]

It will be noticed that the substituting of the United States flag is especially included in the disavowal.

---

[1] It is, perhaps, only fair to say that Senator Hoar, who has given a great deal of attention to Hawaiian affairs, and who has discussed them from time to time with great ability, came to a radically different conclusion from that reached by Mr. Foster.

In a debate in the Senate, Jan. 17, 1894, the following remarks occur :

"Senator DANIEL.—I understand the Senator [Mr. Hoar] to say that the United States occupies Hawaii, and raised its flag over the capitol by the invitation of the *de facto* Provisional Government. Now, laying aside the invitation, the question I should like to ask the Senator is, What right had the American minister or the American admiral, at anybody's invitation, to assume the sovereignty of a foreign country in the name of the United States, without the authority of the President or Congress ?

"Senator HOAR.—None at all.

"Senator DANIEL. — And as the Senator has investigated the subject, I should like to ask him, furthermore, what was the condition of affairs brought about by the establishment of the military protectorate over a foreign country in the name of the United States, and if after that the same legal condition existed that existed when there was a *de facto* government.

"Senator HOAR.— There was no such protectorate established; there was no such function assumed; there was no such significance given to the hoisting of the flag. It was an act of courtesy, pure and simple, on the part of the *de facto* Government, as I understand it. It had no more significance than my hanging the United States flag out of my window on the 4th of July when I was travelling in Europe last summer."

This letter from Mr. Foster was written on the 14th day of February. At that time there was about to be sent to the Senate a treaty, in which the Provisional Government, one of the " High Contracting Parties," proposed to cede " absolutely and without reserve to the United States forever all rights of sovereignty of whatsoever kind in and over the Hawaiian Islands and their dependencies, renouncing in favor of the United States every sovereign right of which, as an independent nation, it is now possessed." It would not be right to accuse Mr. Harrison of too careful scrutiny of the circumstances under which this treaty was offered; but the incongruity, not to say absurdity, of professing to make a treaty with a sovereign and independent nation, while that nation's public buildings were occupied by United States troops, and the United States flag was flying over its capitol, in token of what Mr. Foster considered tantamount to the assumption of a protectorate, could not but make itself manifest. Nevertheless, for reasons which are left to conjecture, Mr. Foster did not in so many words order the flag to be taken down; and as Mr. Stevens did not think proper to take the hint so broadly given, nor even thought that his action had been disavowed,[1] the flag con-

---

[1] Mr. Stevens testified as follows:

" The CHAIRMAN. — How long before you received that despatch was it that Admiral Skerrett came ?

" Mr. STEVENS. — I cannot recall.

" The CHAIRMAN. — But it was before you received that despatch disavowing —

" Mr. STEVENS. — I shall object to the term disavowal; I do not admit it was a disavowal."

See also testimony of Mr. McCandless, member of Committee of Safety and Provisional Government:

" Senator FRYE. — Do you know what the estimate of his [Mr. Stevens's] character was among the citizens there ?

" Mr. MCCANDLESS. — I do not know of an American who was not proud of him as a citizen and as the American representative. I happened to have a conversation with him just the day before the flag was taken down; had business with him. I went up to call upon him to talk about some matters. That was the 31st day of March, I think. It was either that or the 30th. At all events it was the day before the flag was taken down. We talked of the situation some, and he stated that he was very well satisfied with everything as it was; and the flag was mentioned, I am quite sure it was among other things, and he said the flag would never come down, and that afternoon or that day, at 11 o'clock, Mr. Blount called on President Dole and said he was going to take the flag down at 4 o'clock that

tinued upon the Hawaiian capitol, and the United States troops remained in possession of the public buildings.

This state of things continued until Mr. Blount came to Honolulu, with the instructions from Mr. Gresham, which have already been referred to. Upon his arrival, having looked the ground over, and for reasons which he sets forth in his report, he thought it proper and expedient and in accordance with his instructions to cause the flag to be hauled down and the troops of the "Boston," with the exception of one company left at the Consulate, to be returned to their ship.

The following is Admiral Skerrett's report to Secretary Herbert in reference to this matter.[70]

U.S.S. "MOHICAN," FLAGSHIP OF THE PACIFIC STATION,
HONOLULU, HAWAIIAN ISLANDS, April 6, 1893.

SIR: Since my last of the 29th ultimo, I have to inform the Department of the arrival, after closing my mail on that day, of the U.S.R.S. "Richard Rush," having on board Special United States Commissioner J. H. Blount. On March 31 I was called by Mr. Blount for a special interview, on which occasion, by his directions, I was ordered to withdraw the "Boston's" force from the shore, and at 11 A.M. on April 1 to haul down the United States flag from the Government building, which was to be replaced by the Provisional Government hoisting the Hawaiian flag. These orders were promptly executed as directed. There was not the remotest evidence shown, by the crowd of natives and others about the Government building, of any feeling; no demonstration of any description. Since which time, by the advice of Mr. Blount, the guard that had been placed at the United States legation was allowed to be returned to that place. This was done to quiet the apprehensions of Minister Stevens. There has been no turmoil of any description on shore; peace and quiet have reigned throughout. The cadets will leave by this steamer, and are ordered to report arrival on reaching San Francisco. The U.S.R.S. "Richard Rush" left for San Diego on the 5th

---

afternoon. Of course, it was very much of a surprise; and it was agreed that the flag should come down the next day.

"Senator FRYE. — Were any demonstrations made at all in taking it down?
"Mr. MCCANDLESS. — No."

instant, after I had had her supplied with eighty tons of coal from the Government coal-pile.

Political affairs remain as formerly stated. I would further state that the " Boston's " force was, before its withdrawal from shore, relieved at the Government building by one company of the Provisional Government's troops.

Very respectfully, your obedient servant,
J. S. SKERRETT,
Rear-Admiral, U.S. Navy,
Commanding U.S. Naval Force, Pacific Station

Hon. SECRETARY OF THE NAVY,

Navy Department, Washington, D.C.

To which may be added a letter to Mr. Blount from Captain Hooper, of the United States Revenue Marine:"

U.S. REVENUE STEAMER " RUSH,"
HONOLULU, April 2, 1893.

Hon. J. H. BLOUNT:

MY DEAR SIR: I witnessed the hauling down of the American flag and the raising of the Hawaiian flag over the Government building at this place yesterday, and was surprised not only at the absence of any indication of the violent and partisan feeling which I had been led to expect, but by the apparent apathy and indifference of the native portion of the assembled crowd, and also their politeness and evident good feeling towards Americans. As I passed freely around among them, accompanied by my son, we were kept busy returning their friendly salutes. The greatest good order prevailed throughout. There were no demonstrations of any kind as the American flag came down, and not a single cheer greeted the Hawaiian flag as it was raised aloft.

The native men stood around in groups or singly, smoking and chatting, and nodding familiarly to passing friends, or leaning idly against the trees and fences, while the women and children who formed a large proportion of the assemblage were talking and laughing good-naturedly. As the hour for hauling down the American flag approached, many people, men and women and children, could be seen approaching the Government square, in a most leisurely manner, and showing more interest in the gala-day appearance of the crowd than in the restoration of their national flag. The air of good-natured indifference and idle curiosity with which the native men regarded the proceedings, and the presence of the women and children in their white or bright-colored dresses, was more suggestive of a country "fair" or horse-race than the sequel to a "revolution."

Even the presence of the "armed forces" of the Provisional Government, numbering perhaps two hundred, parading the corridors of the Government house, failed to elicit any sign of a feeling of anger or resentment. In half an hour after the exchange of flags had been made, the crowd had dispersed and only the "force" of the Provisional Government, which I was told was necessary to prevent mob violence, remained to indicate that a "revolution" had recently taken place. While among the crowd I looked carefully for indications of "arms" upon the person of the natives, but saw none, although with the thin clothing worn by them the presence of a revolver or such an arm could easily have been detected.

If any danger of mob violence on the part of the natives existed, all outward signs of it were carefully concealed. Only evidences of the greatest good feeling were apparent.

Hoping that this short statement of the facts as they appeared to me may prove of interest to you,

I am, very truly yours,
C. L. HOOPER,
Captain, U.S. Revenue Marine.

This action having been taken, Mr. Cleveland was made the object of attacks of the most varied character. The first objection rose to the dignity of a constitutional question. Could Mr. Cleveland order the flag to be taken down at the instance of Mr. Blount? Mr. Stevens, United States minister, might bring the troops on shore and require the flag to be hoisted over the Hawaiian capitol, taking action "tantamount to the creation of a protectorate;" Secretary Foster, in behalf of President Harrison, might disavow this act, and Mr. Stevens might take no notice of such disavowal, and still keep the troops on shore and the flag flying; but could President Cleveland, Commander-in-chief of the United States Army and Navy, order, in the manner he did, his subordinate naval officers to take down the flag and go back on board their ship?

This question cannot be considered here. At first blush it might seem to present no serious constitutional difficulty ; but if the reader wishes to see it discussed in all its bearings, and would like to know what elaborate and ingenious arguments could be urged against the constitutionality of this action, he has only to consult the congressional records during the early part of the year 1894.

If such things were interesting, some very curious comments made by Mr. Cleveland's opponents and the Republican press might be quoted here. One main suggestion, upon which the changes were rung in every possible way, was that the taking down of the flag was, and was intended by Mr. Cleveland to be, an invitation to overturn the Provisional Government. But in view of the letters of the United States officers above quoted, and as the facts became better known, the futility of such a charge came gradually to be recognized, and the ground was taken that it was a bitter disgrace to the American people that the flag of the United States should ever have been lowered from the Hawaiian capitol, under any circumstances whatever.

"This is the first time in thirty years," said Senator Davis, of Minnesota, in a debate on Hawaiian affairs in January, 1894, "that an American flag has been lowered by an American hand, under circumstances which brought a feeling of shame and dishonor to the American heart."

Mr. Blair in the House of Representatives, in February, 1894, said that the first action of Commissioner Blount on arriving at Honolulu was to give an order to haul down the American flag.

"Why, Mr. Speaker," he said, "I had grown into the idea that the American ensign could not be hauled down. In times past an order had been given, under other circumstances, ' to shoot any man who attempts to haul down the flag.' "

If taken down at all, so argued one leading and influential newspaper of the day, the flag should have been hauled down at sunset in the usual course, and not have been hoisted again in the morning. In other words, an act which might be right in itself, should not be done publicly and in the face of day. The idea that the United States flag, once raised as an act of sovereignty, should never be pulled down, whether flying rightfully or wrongfully, survives and is inculcated at the present day, with what result to the principles and morals of the country the moralist must decide.[1]

Other singular comments upon this whole Hawaiian affair might be presented. One or two may be reproduced here by way of illustration. Thus, Mr. Boutelle, in a debate in the House of Representatives on the 10th of August, 1894, referring to resolutions for recognition of the republic of Hawaii, remarked:

The mere formal performance of a duty, on the part of the Executive, which ought to have been performed long since — the fact that the administration has performed this duty reluctantly, haltingly, grudgingly, and secretly — does not relieve us from our responsibility or our duty. The outrage upon every principle of public honor that has characterized the so-called "Hawaiian policy" from the beginning has been carried fittingly to the end; and every principle of international probity, every idea of national dignity, every sentiment of public honesty, and every impulse of American manhood has been trampled under foot by this administration.

Senator Cullum, of Illinois, in a speech in the Senate in January, 1894, on Hawaiian affairs, expressed himself as follows:

---

[1] As late as March of the current year a leading journal of New York, in an article purporting to sum up in an impartial manner the chief acts of Mr. Cleveland's administration, says:

"In the Hawaiian matter he offended the national sentiment. His order to haul down the American flag, and his attempt to use the bayonets of our marines to restore a preposterous Queen to an overturned throne, were acts distinctly hostile to American ideas."

Where is the living man whose very heart has not swelled with indignation as he has witnessed the perpetration of inexcusable and unprecedented outrages upon a weak and struggling people? Outrages which, unjust and immoral as they were towards that little band, were a thousand times more disgraceful and immoral against our own American citizenship. The shield and panoply of honor, which has shone like a star over the pathway of American glory, has been blackened and tarnished, while our entire people are doing the penance of humiliation and shame.

But the above products of our colder clime seem almost prosaic, when the refusal of the Provisional Government to accept Mr. Willis's peaceful overtures becomes transmuted and, as it were, idealized in the richer and more exuberant imagination of the tropics.

In a speech at Honolulu upon the first anniversary of the Provisional Government, Mr. Walter G. Smith offers the following tribute to his fellow-countrymen. After drawing a parallel between the fight at Bunker Hill and the proceedings at the time of the dethronement of the Queen, he goes on to say:

It must ever be remembered that your defiance to the tottering Hawaiian monarchy lost no tone of sternness or of courage when you stood at bay to the President of the United States and the power which he misused. There is nothing more inspiring in the annals of 1776 than the unwavering front which you preserved in your great emergency. There, on the one side, was the chief of sixty millions — here was an armed body of a paltry thousand; there was the strongest of modern powers, with its army and its fleets — here were a few lone rocks in the ocean without a fort upon their pinnacles and without a gun upon a deck; there was a great Government whose President had declared that our dethroned Queen should reign again — here was a little band of men who said that she must pass over their dead bodies first; there in our harbor were the broadsides of a possible foe — here on shore was a battalion behind its sand-bags! The odds were great, but the patriots of Hawaii took them; and if the American people, aroused by that spectacle, had not placed themselves between us and all harm, I feel that here upon this soil would have been a new Thermopylæ, not less consecrated to human courage than was that which made immortal the memory of 300 Greeks.

It is, of course, fortunate that the American people interposed to frustrate Mr. Cleveland's sanguinary designs; but one cannot help feeling that, by so doing, they may have prevented an exhibition of heroic and inspiring self-sacrifice which the world could ill afford to lose.

APPENDIX.

It may be permitted to say a few words about the present Government of the Sandwich Islands, which calls itself republican.

About a year after the establishment of the Provisional Government, the work of framing a constitution was entered upon, and a convention was called for that purpose.

Only those who were willing to take an oath to support the Government and oppose the reëstablishment of the monarchy were permitted to vote for the members of this assemblage. About 3,200 were registered and voted.

The task before the convention was not an easy one, because it was necessary, under the forms of republicanism, to establish and perpetuate the rule of the Provisional Government and its adherents over a population of 90,000, of which the American numbered only about 2,000.

But hope of present annexation had been given up, and the convention having met, a constitution was presented and adopted, and in July, 1894, was promulgated; the new name thought proper to be given to the country being the "Republic of Hawaii."

To know what a republic is according to the views which obtain in this country, it may be convenient to turn to the constitution of Massachusetts. In this instrument we find, Article 5:

All powers residing originally with the people, and being derived from them, the several magistrates and officers of government vested with authority, whether legislative, executive, or judicial, are their substitutes and agents, and are at all times accountable to them.

And again, Article 7:

Government is instituted for the common good, for the protection, safety, prosperity, and happiness of the people, and not for the profit, honor, or private interest of any one man, family, or class of men.

Therefore the people alone have an incontestable, unalienable, and indefeasible right to institute the government, and to reform, alter, or wholly change the same, when their protection, safety, property, and happiness require it.

Under the constitution of Hawaii there are two Chambers, a Senate and House of Representatives, each consisting of fifteen members. Senators are chosen for six years, Representatives for two years. The Legislature meets once in two years, but the session cannot extend over more than sixty days, without the consent of the President. The latter is elected by vote of the two Houses sitting together, but the majority must include a majority of the Senate.

Male citizens twenty years of age, who can fluently speak, read, and write either the English or Hawaiian language, can vote for Representatives. Those are also admitted to the franchise who have special letters of denization, entitling them to all the privileges of Hawaiian citizenship, without their being required to renounce allegiance to their native government. Many American residents of the Sandwich Islands hold such letters.

The qualification of voters for members of the Senate are the same as those for Representatives, with the addition of a property requirement. Thus the voter for members of the Senate must be either in receipt of a money income of $600, or must be able to show either that he possesses real estate in the republic worth $1,500, or that he has personal property of not less than $3,000.

In order to be a member of the House, a person must be in receipt of an income of $600, or must own property worth $1,000. A Senator must be a property-owner to the extent of $3,000, or must be in receipt of an income of $1,200.

A very important feature of this constitution is the establishment of a body entitled the Council of State, consisting of fifteen members, five of whom are appointed by the President, and five elected by each branch of the Legislature.

It will be seen that this body is not in touch with the voters at any point, but its powers are very extensive. The President and Cabinet, constituting the Executive Council, may at any time, when the Legislature is not sitting, call together the Council of State for special advice, and in time of emergency may upon the request of the President and Cabinet appropriate public money, thus acting with all the authority of the supreme law-making body.

To obtain naturalization, a man must possess property worth $200, must renounce all foreign allegiance, and he must come from a country with which Hawaii has a naturalization treaty.

This constitution was never submitted to the people or any portion of them for their approval.

The President of the republic, as above related, is elected for a term of six years. In the present instance the formality of an election was dispensed with, and Mr. Dole was appointed by the convention President for the first six years.

The power to do this was nowhere granted to the convention, which was chosen simply for the purpose of framing a constitution. It took the power into its own hands, and there has been no pretence of submitting this appointment to an assent or ratification of the Legislature or of the people, in any form whatever.

According to the census of 1890, the people of Hawaii at that time numbered about 90,000, of these about 35,000 were natives, 6,000 half-caste, 7,500 American and English descent, 15,000 Chinese, 13,000 Japanese, 8,500 Portuguese, 2,000 Americans, 1,400 British, 600 Polynesians, 250 Norwegians, 70 French, and some 400 other foreigners. The native population is now probably less than 30,000.

How can it be said that the Government of Hawaii is republican in any such sense as we use this term, or that it has anything in common with the Governments of our Union, State or National?

Mr. Z. S. Spalding, formerly a confidential agent of the United States State Department, afterwards in the war lieutenant-colonel of the Twenty-seventh Ohio Regiment, and in 1894 a sugar planter on an extensive scale, stated the following opinions before the congressional committee: [72]

Senator GRAY. — You do not think a republic would be a good form of government for the people of that country who are now entitled to suffrage?

Mr. SPALDING. — No.

Senator FRYE. — With the suffrage practically universal?

Mr. SPALDING. — Not as it is now, under the constitution of 1887.

Senator GRAY. — Would you think the outlook for a republican form of government better if the right of suffrage were more extensive?

Mr. SPALDING. — No; I should think that the people there, from the circumstances surrounding them, are not favorable to a republican form of government. There is not enough interest in the country for a republic — there are too many waves of prosperity and depression.

Senator FRYE. — Suppose there were a limit to the suffrage?

Mr. SPALDING. — If you were to limit the suffrage, then you might have a government which would, in my opinion, be safe and advisable in the proportion that it would be limited.

Senator FRYE. — But that would not be a government of the people?

Mr. SPALDING. — It would not.

Senator GRAY. — The more narrow the suffrage, the more stable the government?

Mr. SPALDING. — Yes, because these people are like a good many in the United States — better governed than governing.

Senator GRAY. — They need to be governed?

Mr. SPALDING. — I think so.

The CHAIRMAN. — What do you think of the future success of Hawaii as a government, having reference to the welfare of all classes in that country, if that government — taking the constitution of 1887 as a basis — should be placed in the hands of a native Kanaka dynasty?

Mr. SPALDING. — If it were placed in the hands of a native Kanaka dynasty it would probably run back to where it was when Captain Cook visited it.

The CHAIRMAN. — You think those people need to be under control?

Mr. SPALDING. — While the King has been on the throne the brains of the white man have carried on the government.

Senator GRAY. — You think they need an autocratic government?

Mr. SPALDING. — We have now as near an approach to

autocratic government as anywhere. We have a council of fifteen perhaps, composed of the business men of Honolulu — some of them workingmen, some capitalists, but they are all business men of Honolulu. They go up to the Palace, which is now the official home of the Cabinet, — they go up there perhaps every day and hold a session of an hour to examine into the business of the country, just the same as is done in a large factory or on a farm.

Senator GRAY. — They control the government?

Mr. SPALDING. — They control it. They assemble — "Now it is desired to do so and so; what do you think about it?" They will appoint a committee, if they think it necessary, or they will appoint some one to do something, just as though the Legislature had passed a law to be carried out by the officers of the people.

As a supplement to this, a passage is cited from a letter written to the New York "Tribune," in 1894, by Mr. Gorham D. Gilman, the able and vigilant representative of the Hawaiian Government in this country:

The men at the head of affairs in Hawaii at the present time are largely descendants of Americans, most of them born on the islands. They have but one object in view — that of endeavoring to found a government upon the principles which actuated the patriots of the United States. They have taken their lessons of jurisprudence from the constitutional laws which govern New England. They are impressed by the same lofty ideas of personal liberty; they are endeavoring to establish a government of the people, for the people, and by the people, and although the Hawaiian race is not largely active in participating in the formation of this government, yet it is confidently expected that the day is not far distant when they will cheerfully fall into line, and accept the condition of affairs as vastly better for their interests than those preceding the revolution of July, 1893.

To which it may be added, that whether the Hawaiian race fall into line cheerfully or mournfully, they must in either event accept such condition of affairs as their rulers, in pursuance of their lofty ideals, may see fit to impose upon them.

REFERENCES TO CONGRESSIONAL REPORT.

No.	Page.	No.	Page.	No.	Page.
1	1100	25	1591	49	1054
2	1123	26	1523	50	1054
3	1156	27	1033	51	473
4	1161	28	1776	52	473
5	1185	29	581	53	1205
6	1196	30	1313	54	1032
7	1210	31	1394	55	1046
8	1162	32	576	56	631
9	1036	33	1198	57	1027
10	1769	34	1415	58	1206
11	448	35	1400	59	1012
12	452	36	1045	60	1993
13	1769	37	1006	61	2126
14	1773	38	1337	62	2087
15	1864	39	1397	63	2087
16	618	40	1527	64	1245
17	448	41	1337	65	1266
18	336	42	1331	66	2115
19	1846	43	1195	67	2128
20	1867	44	1415	68	2129
21	543	45	2125	69	1989
22	639	46	483	70	2211
23	1346	47	413	71	1870
24	599	48	2209	72	256